BRITAIN'S RUGBY GROUNDS

A guide to 50 rugby union grounds in Britain

CHRIS HARTE

First published in Great Britain in 2003 by
League Publications Ltd
Wellington House
Briggate
Brighouse
West Yorkshire HD6 1DN

A CIP catalogue record for this book is available from the British Library

ISBN 1-901347-11-7

Printed and bound in Great Britain

Written & edited by Chris Harte
Designed, typeset & produced by Graham Clay
Ground detail researched by Paul English
Pictures sourced by Andy Howard
Photographers: SW Pix, Paul Wickson, Dave Williams, Huw Evans, Fotosport, Andy Howard, Steve Ward,
Phil Harvey, Guy Pedliham, Steve Barber, Action Images, Nottingham Evening Post, Neale Harvey,
Nick Melton, Ian Summers, Gordon Mather, Jordan at Coventry RFC, Steve Mitchell

CHRIS HARTE has been writing and reporting on sport for nearly thirty years but this is his first book solely devoted to rugby union. His other titles have concentrated on cricket, football and sports journalism.

His initial cricket book, 'The Fight for The Ashes,' was published in 1982, and in 1987 he won his first literary award, for the highly-acclaimed 'The History of The Sheffield Shield.' Two years later he again won literary recognition for 'Two Tours and Pollock,' the story of an Australian cricket tour of South Africa.

His last major cricket work, 'A History of Australian Cricket', was first published in 1993, and has proved to be so popular that a new revised edition has recently been printed.

During the 1990s he wrote four distinctly esoteric books on the life of a sports journalist, which included all the daily trials and tribulations of running a sports reporting service.

His connection with 'Rugby Times' needs no explanation, although he is still a senior partner in 'National Sports Reporting,' the London based sports agency.

Chris Harte has been married for so long he has forgotten the names of most of the people who attended his wedding. He, his wife and their cat live in both London and Yorkshire.

His next book, due out in twelve months time, will be an in depth study of sporting magazines from 1792 to 1926.

THERE are many people and organisations who have helped both directly and indirectly in the making of this book, most of which first appeared in *Rugby Times* and I am sincerely grateful to them all.

At club level many people gave me help and information but those who deserve special mention include George Clark (Boroughmuir), Graham Currier (Wharfedale), Roy Guy (Harrogate), Phil Harvey (Cambridge University), Stuart Henderson (Melrose), Jack Kay (Blackheath), John Lowe (Doncaster), Bill McMurtrie (Glasgow), Peter Millard (Stourbridge), Allan Price (London Welsh), Sam Rossiter-Stead (Leicester), John Shotton (Tynedale) and Mike Smith (Halifax).

There has been in-house support at both the organisations whose offices I inhabit, namely *Rugby Times* (in Yorkshire) and National Sports Reporting (in London). The Cardiff-based Westgate Sports Agency must also be thanked for providing information.

I have tapped the minds of many of my colleagues for news, comment, historical fact and opinion. They include Andrew Baldock *(Press Association)*, Steve Bale *(Daily Express)*, Paul Bolton *(Daily Telegraph)*, Julian Easterbrook *(Middlesex Chronicle)*, Brendan Gallagher *(Daily Telegraph)*, Graham Gillespie *(Rugby News)*, Geoff Green *(Manchester Evening News)*, David Hallett *(Cambridge Evening News)*, Dave Hammond *(Glasgow Herald)*, David Hands *(The Times)*, Alan Hedley *(Newcastle Journal)*, Andy Howell *(Western Mail)*, Michael Knox *(Oxford Mail)*, Bill Lothian *(Edinburgh Evening News)*, John Wilkinson *(Coventry Evening Telegraph)* and Sarah Niblock *(Scottish Rugby Union)*.

Naturally there have been many others who have taken an interest as the series unfolded each week in *Rugby Times* and it is obviously impossible to mention them all.

However, I cannot forget the enthusiasm shown by some people at the thought of their club being mentioned in a national rugby newspaper especially the ladies in the Grove Park Grill at Manchester Rugby Club, committeemen at Melrose through to the chef at Wakefield.

Thank you all.

Launched in September 2002, *Rugby Times* is Britain's only weekly publication dedicated to rugby union and has rapidly established itself as a major player.

Published every Friday as a quality tabloid-sized newspaper, it provides comprehensive coverage of the international, national and local game. Whilst news led, there is also full coverage of every Premiership and National League match, plus in-depth features, comment and analysis. It also provides six pages of results, tables, fixtures and statistics - the most thorough service of its kind.

Rugby Times is available from all good newsagents, or by subscription. For further information, call 01484 404920 or visit www.rugbytimes.com

Contents

AS the sport of rugby union continues to pull in more spectators, traditional rugby grounds at the highest level of the professional club game have become a dying breed. Increased spectator numbers and the introduction of specific ground criteria to cater for a more expectant audience has led to a situation where much of the existing stadia had become out of line with modern day demands. Sale Sharks, having outgrown their homely Heywood Road base, will now be sharing Edgeley Park with Stockport County FC in the 2003/04 season and Bristol's relegation from the Premiership means that only half of the top flight teams have homes whose sole purpose is rugby.

This book fills two major needs. It gives a comprehensive account of how those clubs forced into change have coped with the demands of the modern era while also giving a fascinating insight into those grounds up and down the country as yet untouched by the clamour for plastic bucket seats and corporate car parking. Chris Harte unearths such gems with their associated oddities by taking on the role of historian, nostalgist, navigator, food critic and friend of the people.

Comprehensive directions to each ground and associated facts make 'Britain's Rugby Grounds' essential for reference purposes but it is Chris Harte's rhetoric that elevates the title to must-have status, whether you are a devotee of rugby union or simply a seeker of truth and justice.

The disparity between professional club rugby and 'community' club rugby has never been greater, but some things remain constant. A rude steward is a rude steward and a dodgy pie is a dodgy pie no matter the surroundings and the author pulls no punches when standards are found to be sloppy on his visit to 50 selected grounds up and down the length of the UK. His attempts to escape the clutches of secret police stewards, his immediate dislike to instant coffee and near-death brushes with boy-racers masquerading as players at Sedgley Park make for a riotous read.

Rugby's success in the past has been to provide a convivial atmosphere; striking the balance between ensuring that sentiment remains alive and well and providing up-to-date facilities without over-sanitization may seem small fry, but it's at the very essence of what club rugby should be about. Chris Harte captures it perfectly.

Jon Newcombe
Editor, Rugby Times

WHEN the concept of Rugby Times was first being discussed in detail, around the dinner table of a public house on Emley Moor, one of the ideas for a regular feature centred around rugby grounds.

Very few people seemed to have any idea about the quality of spectator comforts being offered, nor where some clubs were even situated. It was soon decided that I would take on the task of trying to visit as many grounds as possible and to report on what I had found.

In our first issue, published in September 2002, I described my intentions in the following terms:

"For years, as the game existed in its sham-amateurism, at one level, and its muddied-oafs perception at another, grounds were generally little short of mounds of mud-heaps for the paying spectator. In fact rugby was languishing in the Stone Age of spectator sport.

While the game was as enjoyable and competitive as anywhere in the world, the appalling state of many grounds was dragging the sport down. With the famous 'blazers' attitude either helpless or uncaring or, worse, class-ridden, numerous clubs took the loyalty and support of their spectators for granted. They offered derisory facilities, average catering and primitive viewing conditions. Many had no programme or team-sheet for their paying customers and the thought of providing a toilet around the ground for women was unthinkable.

But, thank goodness, much has changed within the game over the last decade or so and because of this we feel that a survey of the new facilities is long overdue.

However, we shall tell the truth in our reports. If grounds are difficult to find or enter, if car parks are a bog, staff are surly and bars unwelcoming, then why should anyone go to a game when the leisure alternatives are so many and varied? Similarly, programmes must offer more than a list of players and the public address system (if audible in today's loud, shouting culture) should be telling people what they can do, not what they cannot.

Our aim is to see if the experience of our selected club is one to endure or to enjoy. Perspective will be maintained regarding size and resources but if facilities inevitably are more lavish at Leicester than at Old Rubberduckians, the same standards will be applied to comfort, competence and customer care. Each of the grounds will be marked out of ten on each of ten categories, ranging from ease of access to attitude of staff to quality of food and drink.

The appeal of the club shop and selection of goods available, ability to view the match and the aesthetic pleasures will all be judged, leading to a total mark out of one hundred."

I started off in August at Wakefield in West Yorkshire and finished with a round fifty at Stourbridge in South Staffordshire on the last day of the regular season in late April.

What I found ranged from the superb organisation at Worcester to the disgraceful Meadowbank Stadium in Edinburgh. The extreme difference between these two grounds shows that the game still needs to be kicked along in certain quarters.

In general terms, and at the lower level of the game, it certainly appeared that clubs in the north of England provided better facilities, finer food and friendlier company than some of those in the south. Scotland and Wales were different still in that clubs were far more an integral part of the community.

As the features have been published in Rugby Times so clubs have reacted with either complete fury or with telephone calls of profuse thanks. Quite a number now have the article about their club in a frame on a wall of their clubhouse: others try to forget I ever paid them a visit.

Some clubs, particularly Leicester, went out of their way to give me access to every nook and cranny of the Welford Road ground on a very busy day. Others tried to make my job as difficult as possible by either getting stewards to trail me (and threatening to remove me from the ground if I dared step out of line) to following my every move on closed circuit television.

Many wanted me to write about "our plans for future development." This, of course, would not have reflected on the true nature of the current situation from the eyes of a punter who had paid his money at the gate.

Fortunately I had discussed this planned series at length with Alan Lee of The Times who had had the initial idea of reviewing venues in the first place. His articles on racecourses and cricket grounds have been acclaimed in many quarters and on his return visits to racecourses he can now comment on any progress made since his initial assessment.

I must thank Alan, not only for his encouragement in attempting this on-going series, but also for allowing me to copy a number of his rating criteria.

As soon as I started visiting clubs in the lower echelons of the English league system, I found club men and women who were just delighted to have a sports writer at their club. "No one from a national publication has ever visited us before," was said to me so often it became a slight embarrassment.

What so many of them also failed to realise was that their homeliness and goodwill so often left me with a warmth towards them, even if I had criticised some of their facilities in my copy.

I criss-crossed Britain over an eight-month period to get these first fifty ground reports available for book form. I have already started on a second series. However, it is the breadth and depth of the game which surpasses anything I had previously imagined. Rugby is everywhere.

So, too, are the kitchens which each week see battalions of mainly female helpers providing food for those muddied oafs or their camp followers. Quite unofficially, and with absolutely no parameters to follow, I have also judged these fifty clubs by the quality and standard of their sausages. The winner is Richmond, closely followed by London Welsh and Wakefield. Any new recommendations will be rapidly assessed.

Chris Harte
London, July 2003

Ground Rankings

Ground	Score	Rank	Page
Worcester	91%	1st	215
Leicester	88%	=2nd	99
Melrose	88%	=2nd	127
Wharfedale	86%	4th	211
Northampton	85%	5th	143
Richmond/London Scottish	83%	6th	171
Waterloo	82%	7th	207
Otley	80%	8th	155
London Welsh	79%	=9th	115
Sedgley Park	79%	=9th	191
Harlequins	78%	=11th	79
Llanelli	78%	=11th	103
Newcastle	78%	=11th	139
Gloucester	77%	=14th	71
Newbury	77%	=14th	135
Blackheath	76%	=16th	27
Doncaster	76%	=16th	55
Manchester	75%	18th	123
Cambridge University	74%	=19th	47
Harrogate	74%	=19th	83
London Irish	73%	=21st	107
Tynedale	73%	=21st	199
Bedford	72%	23rd	23
Bath	71%	=24th	19
Halifax	71%	=24th	75

Ground	Score	Rank	Page
Lydney	71	=24th	119
Glasgow	70	=27th	67
Pontypridd	70	=27th	167
London Wasps	70	=27th	111
Bridgend	69	=30th	39
Orrell	69	=30th	151
Leeds	68	=32nd	95
Sale	68	=32nd	183
Coventry	67	=34th	51
Jed-Forest	67	=34th	87
Boroughmuir	66	=36th	31
Esher	66	=36th	63
Kendal	66	=36th	91
Oxford University	65	=39th	159
Stourbridge	65	=39th	195
Rosslyn Park	62	=41st	175
Saracens	62	=41st	187
Bristol	61	=43rd	43
Nottingham	61	=43rd	147
Wakefield	60	45th	203
Bracknell	59	=46th	35
Plymouth Albion	59	=46th	163
Neath	54	48th	131
Rotherham	53	49th	179
Edinburgh	37	50th	59

Recreation Ground, Bath, Somerset, BA2 6PW.

THE approach to Bath has always been chaotic in these modern times of overcrowded roads. It has improved somewhat from the north in recent years with the building of a new road upon the hill towards Gloucester but what it was like prior to the advent of the motorway beggars belief. The old A4, going from London to Avonmouth, still wends its way around the narrow streets.

When the architect and town planner John Nash first designed, and supervised erecting, his palladian style buildings the town became known for his creation. He had already developed Regent Street, Regent's Park and Marble Arch in London, and Bath became an extension of his talent. Well-to-do people flocked to stay in the town and to dip into the spa waters. By the 1850s the name Bath meant quality.

Little has changed from Nash's grand plan although modernisation has seen some alterations to the town centre. The Abbey, Art Gallery and Museum are still focal points for tourists as are the Roman Baths. The River Avon gushes over a weir by Pulteney Bridge and on its western side is the Recreation

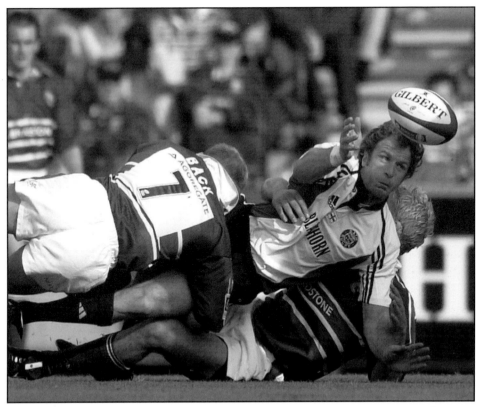

Ground, home of Bath Rugby Football Club.

One of the shops on the bridge, which is actually Argyle Street, is called 'Bath Rugby' and is open six days a week. It is the club shop and its whole persona oozes status and quality. Here is where you buy your club embossed track-suits, polo neck sweaters, hats, gloves, shirts and other like clothing. There is no tat in this shop which always appears to be crowded, especially with fathers buying something for their sons. On match days there is a mobile shop inside the ground.

Car parking is strictly limited.

Some two hundred match day passes are issued for the William Street entrance with other arrangements made with nearby sporting clubs to use their facilities. Otherwise it is street parking some distance away: such are the problems of having a city centre site.

Having been granted parking permission, I left my vehicle and wandered into the cricket pavilion which has multiple matchday use. This is where the journalists, photographers and stewards congregate and I just happened to notice a pile of handbooks on the tea-room counter. Thinking they were media handouts I took one and sat down with a hot drink to read it through.

What I had took me by complete surprise. I had no idea that you could get a 'Diploma in Stewarding' which, so I read, "... could lead to a Degree," in the subject. Initially I thought this was a joke until I read on. What I had was titled: 'NVQ Level 2 Candidate Pack' and was a 208 page document for the stewarding exam "in 310 Units" issued by the Telford College of Arts & Technology.

"You're not supposed to be reading that," said a voice. I looked up and found that a group of stewards had come in and seen what I had in my hand. After assuring them that I had no evil intent, I asked how many of them were taking the exams. All were, with one twenty-something female telling me: "I really, really feel that I have the talent for a career in stewarding. I really, really know that I can relate to people."

With my folder in hand I walked around the ground much to the disquiet of those watching my movements on CCTV from the control box. What I can say is that she was really, really useless at following me and it took one of her colleagues to keep checking my 'access all areas' pass to make sure I had not strayed into forbidden territory.

The ground has a capacity of 8200, and within such a restricted area the facilities on offer are as good as would be expected. Each corner of the ground has an entrance with stewards checking tickets. No money is taken on the gates as every match is all-ticket.

The main Blackthorn Stand is an established structure which has 2044 seats with the press and control boxes on the roof. The view from the front press seats is superb: where else in the county would you get such a vista running from the palladian on your left, around to Bathwick on the hill over the Kennett & Avon Canal, and on the far right the dwellings of Widcombe. The distraction is all encompassing.

Back in the ground there are three further sides: the south end is now known as the Hamptons International Stand and has twenty-eight corporate suites capable of accommodating 560 guests.

Underneath is an excellent section for disabled fans and their carers. The centre of the East Stand holds 2212 spectators in uncovered seating: it might be awful on a wet day but the compensation must be the splendid view of Bath Abbey in all of its glory. Standing sections make up the rest of the spectator viewing areas.

It is behind the North Stand where most of the action is to be

BATH 71%

How the Rec rates...

Access:	7
Car Parking:	5
Staff Attitude:	6
Comfort & Cleanliness:	6
Programme:	8
Catering:	7
Scenery & Surroundings:	10
Bars:	7
Club Shop:	9
Viewing & Shelter:	6
Total:	71 %
Ranking	=24th

ADDRESS: Recreation Ground, Bath, Somerset, BA2 6PW

DIRECTIONS: A Park & Ride at Lambridge (Bath Rugby's training ground) is open for all 1st XV weekend fixtures. From M4 (Junction 18) follow the A46 to Bath, after the first set of lights the Lambridge Park & Ride is immediately on the left. If travelling direct to the ground follow the above directions but continue on the A46 and follow the signs to Bath City Centre, from where the Recreation Ground is well signposted.
By rail, from Bath Spa Station walk up Manvers Street towards town centre. Turn right into North Parade and left down steps.

PARKING: No public parking at the ground.

TELEPHONE: 01225-325200

FAX: 01225-325201

TICKET DETAILS: 01225-460588

CLUB SHOP: 01225-311950

WEBSITE: www.bathrugby.co.uk

found. Although there are bars and catering points all around, it is here where the locals know the two refreshment areas for the best selections. 'The Hut' opens on to the downstairs concourse while in the clubhouse 'The Hatch' serves hungry drinkers. The main bar has all expected facilities with views of the ground for those who stay out of the cold.

Along the walkway are some trestle tables where the Bath Rugby Supporters' Club have their stall. As well as taking coach bookings for future away games they sell their own souvenirs and other ephemera.

The programme is of sixty-four pages, a quarter of which are advertisements. It is an informative production, heavily illustrated and containing lots of colour. The Supporters' Club pages were especially good.

There are supposed to be plans afoot to extend the capacity at the Rec. Whatever happens I just hope that the rugby atmosphere which the ground exudes stays as good as always.

Goldington Road, Bedford, MK40 3NF.

BEDFORDSHIRE is a flat county. You notice it more so as the Midland Mainline train from London leaves the congestion which is Luton and heads north. A glimpse here and there of the M1 motorway; through stations with names such as Leagrave, Harlington and Flitwick; past vast open pits, and brickworks with their chimneys working overtime.

The town of Bedford on a bitter winter's day can produce a wind-chill factor many degrees below freezing. The numbing cold has meant that the walk through the northern part of the business area to the rugby ground has been a task in itself.

In fact the walk is fascinating. First you come across Bedford Modern School, a rugby hotbed if ever there was one. The early twentieth century sports writer, one

Edward Humphrey Dalrymple Sewell, has penned numerous stories about rugby at his school and at Bedford Rugby Football Club. Many of his Edwardian heroes have their pictures on the walls around the clubhouse.

Then there is the outstanding architecture of the High School for Girls after which are the imposing walls of Bedford Prison. Further along are Alms Houses, soon to be renovated for the upwardly mobile, until you arrive at the main reason why the town is so well known: the statue of John Bunyan in St.Peter's Gardens.

His book, The Pilgrim's Progress, written in 1678, still has relevance today. His influence as both author and preacher marked the town out as a centre of Methodism although the current large Italian population has seen a marked shift in religious leanings.

Once the east road splits towards Kimbolton one way and St.Neots the other, the floodlight pylons of the Goldington Road ground come into view. All around the southern flank are offices, many in what were large family homes now converted for business occupation.

To the north of the ground is a hospital, now in disuse. Its design and predominantly Bedfordshire-coloured brick structures overlook the club's northern boundary. Its main use nowadays is to provide two hundred and eighty vehicle spaces on a match day. In between is the rear entrance (which actually has two turnstiles but everyone seems to walk between them) and a further eighty marked car and coach parking areas.

The front gates have turnstiles either side of them with a small match office for collecting tickets. Behind this, inside the gate, is another office now hardly used and one of many reminders of the recent days in which the club played at the top level and needed support staff. Next to it is the hut from which the 'Bedford Rugby Followers Association' operate with their main task being to fill the coaches with supporters going to away matches.

To the right is the main stand with its 1064 wooden seats, most of which are under cover. In front are red bucket seats in a tagged-on section but it is all very user friendly. The original stand was built in 1905 and cost £201. This reconstruction was completed in 1933 and folk lore has it that this was the first rugby ground grand-stand to specifically provide a ladies toilet.

Walking along the eastern boundary brings to the eye a wonderful selection of residences built in bricks of different orange hues. There is only standing accom-modation here until you come to a small building upon which sits the electronic scoreboard. Underneath is a bar and dining-room known as 'The Old Players' Lounge.' The place was completely full which is always a good sign that players stay loyal to a club.

In recent times the northern boundary had been occupied by a huge covered temporary stand and bustling marquees, but they are now gone. The grass has grown back and the whole of the practice pitch can be seen once again. The railings view for spectators is actually quite good and the numbers who congregate along this side of the touchline are substantial.

The Club Shop is situated in one of a number of portakabins sited in the north-west corner astride the driveway towards the back gates. Open every weekday the shop was neatness itself with a selection of items which ranged from shirts, tops, trousers and jerseys in sizes up to XXXL. There were also bags, ties, hats and the usual rugby ephemera.

Opposite the shop are the changing rooms, above which are two of the other bars. The member's area is a large comfortable room capable of holding at least two hundred and fifty. The thing which struck me about it was the clean-liness: the place sparkled. At the far end is the 'Larry Webb Room' with its own private bar and facilities. Here is where the real memorabilia is to be found behind beautifully designed glass cabinet doors.

The main dining area is known as 'Nos's Nosh' and provides excellent lunches albeit at prices slightly higher than to be expected. The outside window-hatch is where other orders are taken and the

BEDFORD   72%

How Goldington Road rates...

Access:	6
Car Parking:	7
Staff Attitude:	9
Comfort & Cleanliness:	8
Programme:	7
Catering:	7
Scenery & Surroundings:	8
Bars:	6
Club Shop:	6
Viewing & Shelter:	8
Total:	72 %
Ranking:	23rd

ADDRESS: Goldington Road, Bedford, MK40 3NF

DIRECTIONS: From M1 (Junction 13) onto A 421. On edge of Bedford join Southern relief road, signposted Cambridge. At roundabout at end of the relief road, turn left to Bedford Town Centre (A428). Continue on Goldington Road, the ground is approx. 4 miles on the right.
Nearest Rail station is Bedford, Midland Road - one mile from the ground.

PARKING: For hospitality only at the ground, but plenty within the old hospital next door.

TELEPHONE: 01234-347980

FAX: 01234-347511

TICKET DETAILS: 01234-347980

CLUB SHOP: 01234-347980

WEBSITE: www.bedfordrugby.co.uk

selection is varied and acceptable. Particularly recommended is the home-made soup. A large burger van provides the children with their greasy food and coloured sugar drinks.

The public bar is in another section of the old clubhouse and the whole area is known as 'Scrum Hall,' a most appropriate name on a busy match day afternoon. Next door are the raised 'Oxford & Cambridge' hospitality suites which offer balcony views overlooking the pitch. These also have bar facilities.

If there is to be a criticism it concerns the use of the public address system where 'Whispering' Sam Roberts stops all conversations in their tracks. During these long pre-match breaks I read the thirty-two page match programme (well edited by the same person) and found it to be a most presentable publication. There is also a club newsletter, 'Follow The Blues' which had information and comment of a most useful nature.

Bedford is a welcoming club and it is always pleasant to visit Goldington Road. In a way I hope they do not get another chance to join the elite of the game for it would only go and spoil what is currently on offer.

A CENTURY or so ago Blackheath was a Kentish village south-east of London in which many of the gentry of the time had their homes. Buildings in the area had been specifically designed by famous architects with the residential centre dominated by Vanbrugh Park.

Long before then, in 1497, the Battle of Blackheath had been fought by Cornish insurgents at exactly the spot which is now the invisible line which marks the Meridian: that is, Greenwich Mean Time. It is called Black-Heath as the actual heath was used, during the black plague, as a burial ground for thousands of Londoners who died during the epidemic. To the north, down the hill in Greenwich Park and by the River Thames, is the Seaman's Hospital. This was where, for two centuries, naval personnel returning from overseas 'adventures' and, having caught venereal disease from various native women, were detained until they were somewhat cured.

The Royal Standard public house, an ancient hostelry, stands at the junction of the Old Dover Road, Vanbrugh Park Road and Charlton Road, along which is the Rectory Field, home of Blackheath Rugby Football Club. The Standard has, on its outside walls, a series of roof to pavement tablets of stone. Engraved on them is the history of the inn and of its huge sporting connections: particularly with reference to early nineteenth century cricket.

More important is the rugby club. It could be argued that without the breakaway from the Football Association, organised by Blackheath and Richmond in 1871, then the Rugby Football Union would not have been formed. Then what? Anyway, it did happen and all followers of the game have 'The Club' as it is colloquially called to thank for the evolution of the game as we know it today.

I have rather a soft spot for the place as generations of my relations used to live in houses nearby and my mother was born in one just over the road. Ninety years ago, so family lore has it, my grandfather used to jump the rear gate in Lizban Street to gain access without paying. I carry on the tradition except I use a press pass instead.

The surrounding area is of medium density housing, a school and blocks of tastefully designed flats. The terraced artisan cottages crowded into streets by the locked western gates used to be sold for a pittance. Nowadays a small three-bedroom home would cost you around £335,000: this has become a very trendy and popular area.

The ground, on a match day, has only one entrance in use. This is the driveway from Charlton Road along which both cars and pedestrians gain their first glimpse of an oasis in the wilderness. There are 115 car parking spaces inside which includes an overflow at the rear in the adjoining Bluecoat School.

A sign on the wall of the first building you come to gives directions to the rugby, cricket, tennis and squash clubs, and, presumably of more importance, the times at which the main club bar is open.

One of the first things which strike you on walking around the ground is the preponderance of litter bins. This is a splendid idea with the result that after a game there is hardly any paper blowing around or rubbish left behind.

The Rectory Field is on high ground overlooking the River Thames. From the main stand on the southern side you can see the towers of Canary Wharf and the top part of The Dome, a useless structure if ever there was one.

Otherwise the views are those of rows of evergreen trees which have been planted systematically around the boundary. They act both as windbreaks and for providing a most pleasant backdrop.

The stand has covered seating for 574 spectators and on each side is medium height concrete terracing which holds another 1123. The three open sides can take another 4300 enthusiasts on various forms of terracing.

Immediately behind the (temporary) western terrace is the cricket square where Kent played county matches until a few years ago. In the 1950s Surrey were regular visitors and the games used to attract very healthy crowds. Further away on this side is the Tennis Club which has five grass and six en-tous-cas courts. The rugby club's floodlit second team pitch is here and they have others in both Charlton Park and Greenwich Park.

The clubhouse has seen a number of extensions over the years but this does not damage the charm and history you feel on walking through its double doors. All around are reminders of the past, with more memorabilia added two years ago when Askeans RFC moved in to share the ground and have a corner of the pavilion as their own.

The Club Shop, as to be expected, offers a wide selection of clothing, ties, badges, track-suits, bags and buttons. Some fleeces fit size XXXXL! The variety of goods showing the club's logo is fairly extensive.

There is one main bar and four smaller ones which are mainly used by sponsors and the committee. The large bar always appears to be crowded but that is mainly due to its user-friendly design. The walls are covered with team photographs and honour boards from all of the four sporting clubs. In the bar used after the game as the players' dining area, the walls have rugby material displayed from the nineteenth century. There were two programmes from home matches played in October 1893, and a montage of rare photographs from 1923 when the then Prince of Wales (Edward VIII) visited for Blackheath's fixture against the New Zealand Maoris.

Catering is provided for virtually all of a match day from a large wooden hut at the side of the clubhouse. The usual fare is on offer but what was so nice was that it was all done with a smile.

Sitting in the pressbox reading your programme prior to a game can be a little difficult as the view and aura is so splendid and distracting. However, the club's thirty-six page publication is a very good effort for this level of the game

How the Rectory Field rates...

Access:	7
Car Parking:	7
Staff Attitude:	10
Comfort & Cleanliness:	8
Programme:	8
Catering:	6
Scenery & Surroundings:	8
Bars:	7
Club Shop:	8
Viewing & Shelter:	7
Total:	76 %
Ranking:	=16th

ADDRESS: The Rectory Field, Charlton Road, Blackheath, London SE3 8SR

DIRECTIONS: The entrance to the Rectory Field is approx. 800 yards from the start of Charlton Road B210 at its junction with Stratheden Road/Westcombe Hill which is a turning off Shooters Hill Road A2. Nearest Railway stations are Blackheath (BR) or Westcombe Park (BR). By Bus - 53 from Central London to Woolwich, 54 from Blackheath (BR), 422 from North Greenwich (Tube) - alight all three services on Charlton Road near the entrance. 108 from North Greenwich (Tube), Blackheath (BR) or Westcombe Park (BR) and alight at the Standard pub - walk along Charlton Road (less than five minutes).

PARKING: 115 parking spaces available at the ground. On-street parking - 2 hours only, free.

TELEPHONE: 020-8293-0853

FAX: 020-8293-0854

CLUBHOUSE: 020-8858-1578

WEBSITE: www.blackheathrugby.co.uk

and provided an excellent amount of information.

The club tried to go professional a few years ago and paid the consequence. Luckily the damage was not irreparable and today it is a thriving place with numerous teams. The welcome is always heartfelt, that is what makes it such a lovely club.

Meggetland, Colinton Road, Edinburgh, EH14 1AS.

FROM the heart of Edinburgh take a brisk walk from Princes Street up the Lothian Road to the famous Bruntsfield Golf Links. Then left along Bruntsfield Place and Colinton Road and on your left will be George Watson's College. A little further south west on the opposite side of the road is Meggetland, home of Boroughmuir Rugby Football Club.

Cross the bridge which sits astride the Union Canal and a short winding track will see you in the car park of Meggetland Playing Fields. The sports played here range from rugby through to rowing, football, tennis and cricket.

The Meggetland Canoe Club occupy the first structure as you enter the grounds with various other sporting clubs sharing the second, larger, adjoining building. Then comes the Boroughmuir RFC clubhouse and changing rooms behind which are numerous tennis courts.

In front of the courts is the ample car park which can easily accommodate all of those wishing to use it on a busy Saturday afternoon. On the day of my visit other than the rugby match there was an East of Scotland Football League game in progress along with ancillary spectators. Everyone parked with ease.

Towards the western end of the grounds was a pavilion and further tennis courts along with an alleyway to the railway station at Slateford. This is where the north-bound trains from London slow to a crawl for their final approach into Edinburgh's Waverley terminus.

There were four football and two rugby pitches in the centre of the playing fields, all of which had seen morning matches. On the northern boundary were the fences, some with individual access gates, of houses and flats from a new residential development called North Meggetland. These were most acceptable properties with, I was told, purchase prices all of which were in six figures.

The rugby ground is fully enclosed with one entrance and its own floodlights. Three sides are grass banking with no cover while the new stand has seats for four hundred under cover. Even though the club are the current Scottish Premier Division champions, their ground is one of the smallest in senior rugby. The capacity is 3500, a figure which has not been reached for some time.

Wherever I went help was always at hand. Club officials were friendly and hospitable, and I probably spoke to all of them. What did surprise me, however, was how many of them had English accents. It was something I would never have contemplated.

The main clubhouse had a large public bar with plenty of seating along with high tables and chairs. The refreshment area, staffed by a group of attractive young women had a large variety of food on offer. I asked why the soup appeared to be a bit on the expensive side and was told that it was because it was genuinely home made. I must confess to have enjoyed a large bowl of a truly magnificent lentil and vegetable offering. You pay for quality and you get it.

In the rear President's Room were stored the items which made up the 'Club Shop' list which appeared in the programme. There is no shop as such but as was pointed out to me the selection of shirts, jumpers, ties, hats, socks and scarves can all be purchased on match day or ordered through the secretary. The programme itself was not a bad effort and obviously was

printed in two sections, the last of which was the team line-up which was completely correct. When did that last happen?

Sitting in the pressbox before the game started was fascinating. A number of people came to say hallo and to chat with local scribes about pieces they had written. No one was critical and it was fairly clear that the home supporters did not come from places now euphemistically known as 'affordable housing areas.'

Behind the southern goal was the smaller of the two clubhouses which, on the day of the match, appeared to be used by committee people and sponsors as a viewing area. Next to it was a scoreboard which was always correct as the man in charge had a clipboard and was recording scores as they happened.

The main view from around the ground was to be enjoyed by those standing behind the northern goal for their panoramic view took in the Braid Hills which were covered in cloud. Along to the right were the Craiglockhart Hills: it was all so tranquil and yet we were in shouting distance of the city centre.

To compare Boroughmuir or any other Scottish rugby club with their English counterparts would be unfair. The culture of the game north of the border is different in many aspects. In some ways the spurning of professionalism within the club game takes one back a couple of decades. That was probably the reason why my visit was so pleasurable.

Lily Hill Park, Bracknell, Berkshire, RG12 2UG.

IN the spring of 1711, Queen Anne was riding through Windsor Great Park, as was her wont, when she realised that the heath land was flat enough for horses to run a considerable distance without stopping. She commanded that the land be cleared and what we now know as Ascot racecourse started its life. Little did she realise that a few hundred yards east would, two and a half centuries later, become the home of Bracknell Rugby Club.

The train journey from London takes just under an hour. After alighting at Martin's Heron station it takes about five minutes walk through a series of alleyways to be in London Road opposite the Running Horse public house.

The area is a complete mixture of new town development and old Berkshire commuter-belt homes. From the station there are three distinct types of property: initially mid-1990s small terrace and detached single frontage houses ideal for young upmarket couples.

Then comes an estate comprising rows of 1960s terraced dwellings centred around cul-de-sacs whose residents have a unified hobby of collecting 1970s cars and parking them on the pavement. After this are quality residences many of which are occupied by management from the nearby RAF Staff College.

Once upon a time these houses strung along London Road would have enjoyed a quiet rural existence. Not any more. The traffic noise reaches high decibel levels as Bracknell has swiftly become the halfway point in the rat-run between the M4 and M3 motorways, especially by those (myself included) who cut ten miles off their journey by using it instead of the congested M25.

Bracknell Rugby Club was formed as recently as 1955, and for seventeen years had their main ground in Eastern Road a few hundred yards away from the present base on the edge of Lily Hill Park. In 1972 they moved in to the newly built clubhouse which had extensions added in 1980 and 1989.

Initially a visit to the ground gives an impression of a number of pitches having been hewn from the woodland which is Bracknell Forest. A walkway over a stream, and by the side of the junior pitch, soon reveals Lily Hill House (now converted to offices) to the north: alas, closer inspection shows up a modern tendency - pollution.

If I was going to be kind I could suggest that the stream and pathways were a new branch of the Tate Modern Gallery in all of its post-modernism glory. There were brown rusting supermarket trolleys; piles of beige coloured cans; plastic bottles, lengths of piping and other discarded items of early twenty-first century life. All were mysteriously covered with a light brown film. Surely the water was impure? Not so, said the locals to whom I popped the question. "It was brown when I played in it as a little girl," said Karen in the office. "It's a natural colour."

Having been put right on that score I walked around the various pitches. A fair bit of effort had gone in to erecting small wooden shelters and placing pine tables and chairs on the low banking. The dugouts on the main pitch were unusual yet attractive but how long they will last before the rot gets into the wood is anyone's guess.

Official figures for the ground's capacity seem to vary from source to source so being an untrained specialist in such matters I made calculations using a rule-of-thumb which would horrify the health and safety experts. The northern boundary with banking could hold fifteen hundred; other standing areas twelve hundred; there were two hundred and forty seats in the temporary stand added to which four hundred could watch from the clubhouse patio and windows: a total of 3,340 spectators.

As I walked towards the stand from the adjoining second team pitch, I realised that a food van of some type was parked by the side. Then I saw the sign which sets every addict's heart speeding: 'Italian Ice Cream,' it read. My pulse started racing: my legs moved more quickly: suddenly I was running: I fell all over the counter: "Vanilla Gelati," I gasped to the women standing staring at me in some sort of bewilderment.

The reply was devastating: my legs buckled: I recoiled as if shot. "Sorry love," came the reply. "It's only burgers today!" I needed to lean on something so went to the nearby rear gate to chat to the committeeman on duty.

His gate was one of three access points into the ground. The main entrance was from the side of the public house with the club having spaces for just fifty-six vehicles. However, in an excellent arrangement with a nearby company, the club have free use of a two-storey car park less than a hundred yards away.

The clubhouse building looks very tired. I was given various reasons as to why it had not been redecorated but in reality they were just excuses. The three unkempt portakabins at the rear and dumped building material in the south-west corner did nothing to enhance the view that there was a lack of attention to detail around the place.

Built on a steep slope, the entrance is on the lower level. Here are the changing rooms and behind a stable door is the club shop. The offerings were poor and nowhere could I find a list of what could actually be obtained.

This laziness extended to the match day programme. Although of fifty-two pages, many were pre-printed and so the death notice of an official has to be repeated in each edition because of reference to him in the president's 'message.' The proof checking is also poor: 'Lilly' for Lily is unforgivable; so is 'Ottley' for Otley. There were others.

The club has three bar areas. One is for use by sponsors and invited guests; the second is for general use while the third is a dining area for when needed. On the day of my visit an urn for hot drinks and three plates of buns and cakes had been set up on a trestle table. This was sufficient for the day's needs, although punters quickly realised that a visit to the outside food van would get them drinks at exactly half the price.

Strangely this is the first rugby club I have visited at which I can recollect seeing a line of one-armed bandits along a bar room wall.

How Lily Hill Park rates...

Access:	6
Car Parking:	8
Staff Attitude:	6
Comfort & Cleanliness:	6
Programme:	4
Catering:	6
Scenery & Surroundings:	7
Bars:	6
Club Shop:	4
Viewing & Shelter:	6
Total:	59 %
Ranking:	=46th

ADDRESS: Lily Hill Park, Bracknell, Berkshire, RG12 2UG.

DIRECTIONS: From M4 (Junction 10) take the A329(M) and follow the signs for Bracknell. Take the B3408 towards Binfield and follow the B3408 over first roundabout, through traffic lights to next roundabout, take third exit signposted Bracknell A329. Follow A329 through next two roundabouts and at third Roundabout take the second exit (Town Centre Bypass). At traffic lights take centre lane and follow signs for A329 Ascot through lights. Over first roundabout and at next roundabout take first exit into Lily Hill Drive. Bracknell RFC is on the right. From M3 (Junction 3) take A322 to Bracknell, then take A332 to Ascot. At Heatherwood Hospital roundabout take first exit (A329) Bracknell and through two sets of traffic lights, over next roundabout, through pedestrian lights. At next roundabout take third exit into Lily Hill Drive. Bracknell RFC is immediately on the right.
Nearest Railway Station is Martin's Heron - the ground is approximately half a mile from the station.

PARKING: Limited at ground but additional parking available nearby.

TELEPHONE: 01344-424013

FAX: 01344-485268

WEBSITE: www.bracknellrugbyclub.com

Club officials were at pains to tell me of their junior, youth and ladies rugby sections, and this I acknowledge. However, a match day spectator would neither know nor probably care of this tireless work. They would come to watch a game at a ground which, quite honestly, could do with some considerable improvement.

The Brewery Field, Tondu Road, Bridgend, CF31 4JE.

THE Vale of Glamorgan has, as its western extremity, the River Ogmore as a boundary. The fast-flowing stream rises in the hills of Mynydd Llangeinwyr, gathering pace and joining other water courses through the steep Vale of Ogmore before hitting the sea near Porthcawl.

The noisy river cuts a deep swathe through the town of Bridgend with the sound of rushing water easily heard from the Market Square. The stone-lined high banking protects the town centre from flooding, although it would take an inundation of biblical proportions to top the embank-ments.

Bridgend is the main town between Swansea and Cardiff, and it was interesting to sit sipping cappuccino in a cafe (actually a gelateria) and listen to the tittle tattle of shoppers. Most preferred to go to Cardiff for their clothes and Swansea for household goods. When I casually asked the couple on my table why they did not shop locally I received a look of horror. "You don't shop for anything important in Bridgend," I was told without any further explanation as if I really knew the answer.

That evening I walked around the pleasant centre of the town. It was then that I started to understand why the earlier comment had been made to me. It is probable that the principal pastime in the area is body-building for it was obvious that the two major industries in the place were in 'security' and as 'bouncers.' What earlier had been a quiet pedestrianised retail precinct was now heaving with crop-haired, tattooed young men shouting loudly and teenage girls drinking beer from bottles before smashing them into thousands of pieces on the brick walkways. The language was unintelligible: maybe it was Welsh.

The spectators attending the Brewery Field, which for all intents and purposes is in a location central to the town, were totally different to those I encountered later. These people were from the abundant village and farming communities which sprawl around this part of the world. Talking to some of them left me with the strong impression that they would scarcely consider venturing "into town" after an evening match.

My understanding of the culture grew as I was taken under the wing of the club's Security Officer who made sure that I saw what I wanted to see and to meet who I wanted to meet. The stewarding, organised by Safestyle Security Crowd Control, was unobtrusive yet visible. It was very well organised and any spectator who needed assistance duly received it.

In the past few years the Brewery Field has undergone extensive refurbishment. Outside the ground over one hundred car parking spaces have been created, while a match-day arrangement with the next door Tesco supermarket has seen further provision organised.

Once inside, the most noticeable structure is the innovative hospitality development. The building, of twenty suites, runs the full length of the eastern side but on a first floor level. This gives shelter to the 3,500 fans who can stand underneath on the terracing in some comfort. Opposite is the clubhouse and grandstand. The ground capacity is 7510, with covered seating for 2823 on three sides.

Access is from three corners of the ground, all of which are situated within easy reach of car parking. Each one has a varying number of turnstiles and all have entry for the

disabled. Just inside the main entrance is the Club Shop. There are a good variety of items for sale, with clothing available in all sizes; many ephemeral goods such as calendars, bags, hats, scarves and, most importantly, large teddy bears wearing club colours.

There have been many improvements to the bar and catering facilities in the clubhouse in recent times. A sit-down meal can be had in Cafe Rooetzo both before and after the game with no need for any pre-booking. The manageress showed me the mouth-watering menu, although the prices were more London than Bridgend. At the other end of the clubhouse, curry meals could be obtained for just £3, while over one hundred guests were

dining upstairs in the President's Suite.

Outside on the terraces was a burger van and a portable carvery. However, there was a distinct lack of ease for a general punter who wanted to obtain a hot drink. They were available, but none in any convenient position.

The bar facilities outside were good and easily accessible. Inside were three major drinking areas, two of which were on the first floor. For some reason most punters tended to be in the crowded ground floor bar while upstairs had plenty of room to spare.

Like most rugby clubs, numerous photographs adorn the clubhouse walls. These ranged from team poses through to a portrait of

BRIDGEND 69%

How The Brewery Field rates...

Access:	9
Car Parking:	9
Staff Attitude:	9
Comfort & Cleanliness:	6
Programme:	4
Catering:	7
Scenery & Surroundings:	4
Bars:	7
Club Shop:	6
Viewing & Shelter:	8
Total:	69 %
Ranking:	=30th

ADDRESS: The Brewery Field, Tondu Road, Bridgend, CF31 4JE

DIRECTIONS: From M4 (Junction 36) take the A4601 to Bridgend town centre. From the town centre take the A4063 signposted Tondu and turn right into Brewery Lane.

Nearest Railway station is Bridgend.

TELEPHONE: 01656-652707

FAX: 01656-656829

WEBSITE: www.bridgendrfc.com

JPR Williams, said to be 'Bridgend's Greatest Player.'

The forty-eight page programme had 22 pages of advertising. Produced by a colourprint agency on behalf of the club, a good half of the adverts had nothing to do with the Bridgend area with some of the proof-checking errors being comical. Incorrect telephone codes were a speciality.

In general a visit to the Brewery Field is a pleasant experience. The club is a friendly concern and my visits there are always enjoyable. It is also nice, after the game, to meet with friendly police who control the traffic splendidly so as to make sure congestion is kept to a minimum.

Then, once we have all gone, it is no doubt batons to the ready for town centre patrols.

THE conurbation known as the city of Bristol has always reminded me of an hermaphrodite: neither one thing or the other.

For a stranger to travel around the ill-marked streets with its poor lighting and strange road markings it is more of a guessing game than an exercise in getting to your intended destination using the shortest possible route.

As a seasoned traveller, I find the thought of going to Bristol for a match, be it football, rugby or cricket, fills me with foreboding.

The chaotic streets of Bombay are far easier to transverse.

Bristol Rugby Football Club is situated in the northern suburb of Horfield. As you approach from the south, using the main Gloucester road, it suddenly dawns on you that outside every shop are concrete bollards.

Some shops have them inside the front windows. I asked a newsagent why they were there and he replied: "We get a lot of ram-raiding around here.

"The kids from the council estate

steal cars, ram them into shop windows and run off with what they can carry. It's a terrible problem so we have to take precautions."

Fortunately the club were kind enough to provide me with secure car parking facilities. For the general punter, who does not qualify for one of the 302 spaces in the large tarmacked area behind the East Stand, it is on-street parking in the nearby maze of houses whose origins appear to be either late-Victorian or jerry-built mid-wars.

As the ground is shared with Bristol Rovers Football Club, it is not surprising that the football mentality spills over into the rugby arena.

I felt sorry for Justin Hopwood, the rugby club's press officer, who kindly gave me an 'all areas access' pass.

As I was conducting this survey he was receiving complaint upon complaint from the section stewards wanting to know what right I had to do such a report.

Their allegations that I was "talking to unauthorised personnel and other people" became more Pythonesque as I walked harmlessly around.

On my return to the spacious press room, situated behind the clubhouse, the poor man was tearing his hair out.

He related the accusations levelled at me which now included the charge of "talking to a barman and function room manager."

I would not have minded these ludicrous allegations except for the fact that not one of them was true. So the warning is: don't aggravate the stewards at Bristol, however innocently.

There are various entrances from the northern end, Filton Avenue, and apparently from Alton Road at the south, although I did not see any of those turnstiles open, and the emergency exits were all bolted shut.

The capacity varies from source to source: The Zurich Premiership Media Guide, Rothmans Football Yearbook, RFU Club Directory and the ground's safety officer all give different figures. The latter's assessment of 11,916 I'll take as true.

Formerly known as 'Buffalo Bill's Field' the ground hosted its first match, against Cardiff, in 1921 with an England v Wales international not long after.

The West Stand is part family enclosure, part general seating and part corporate hospitality. Known as the DAS Stand there are public bars, each with numerous rugby photographs on the walls.

It is clear that Bristol Rovers objected to this for they have put their own illustrations above the rugby ones.

The only problem is that the rugby pictures are framed and of good quality, whereas the football ones are from the 1970s and 80s, torn out of magazines and stuck up with blue-tac!

Then we come to the South Stand. It is a temporary structure of 1,056 seats and sees service at the All England Tennis Championships at Wimbledon each summer.

I hope it is returned clean, for on my visit I was shocked to find it filthy with squashed, putrefying pasties left over from its previous occupants. When I queried this with ground staff I was given preposterous excuses.

As I was walking around I stayed and listened to the Chief Steward (incidentally, a most helpful man) give his briefing.

He said that no child under 14 was to be allowed to sit in the front row of the sponsor's upper seating enclosure. It was an interesting directive.

The large Centenary Stand on the western side seats 1,100 in its upper tier with many more standing on the terraces below.

This is where the broadcasters and journalists are seated in the 'Hill House Hammond' sponsored pressbox.

From there is a superb view over the hills and valleys of suburban Bristol. On a clear day the panoramic scene is intensely detailed.

The ground floor space is used as the 'Bristol Rovers IT Training Centre' in conjunction with Filton College.

The clubhouse is situated at the top of the northern terracing and from it members can obtain an excellent lunch or use the extensive bar area. Although there are bar facilities around the ground this is by far the best of them.

With regard to catering there is a 'Shoguns Restaurant & Bar' on the first floor of the Centenary Stand and on my visit 175 people were being served a splendid lunch.

At each corner of the ground are stalls designated as 'Proper Cornish Pasties.' This naturally begs the question as to what is an improper pasty? However, the product is recommended as being of top value.

The sixty-four page programme contains some worthwhile articles and advertising does not dominate and is sensibly placed so as not to spoil the readers' attention.

Having seen a match-day mobile club shop, I did scour the programme for confirmation of the rumour that there was a shop in the city centre. Alas, I am no wiser.

There was one other publication floating around and that was the 'Bristol Shoguns Supporters Club Newsletter.' It was interesting to read and gave a feeling of a well-supported organisation.

The onus for the upkeep of the Memorial Stadium is not the total

BRISTOL 61%

How the Memorial Ground rates...

Access:	6
Car Parking:	5
Staff Attitude:	3
Comfort & Cleanliness:	4
Programme:	7
Catering:	8
Scenery & Surroundings:	7
Bars:	7
Club Shop:	6
Viewing & Shelter:	8
Total:	61 %
Ranking:	=43rd

ADDRESS: Memorial Stadium, Filton Avenue, Horfield, Bristol, BS7 0AQ

DIRECTIONS: From the North, West and East: Leave M4 (Junction 19) and join the M32. Leave the M32 (Junction 2) and take the third exit signposted Horfield and Southmead. Follow the road (Muller Road) across a roundabout (signposted Memorial Stadium). Continue for approx. 1.5 miles until you come to a set of traffic lights. At this junction turn left into Filton Avenue and the ground is immediately on the left. From the South: Leave M5 (Junction 16) and at the roundabout take the A38 Filton. Travel along the A38 (Gloucester Road) for 4.3 miles. At the set of traffic lights take an unsignposted left turn into Filton Avenue and the ground is on your right.
The nearest mainline rail stations are Bristol Parkway or Bristol Temple Meads.

PARKING: Limited at the ground - plenty of on-street parking nearby.
TELEPHONE: 0117-311-1461
FAX: 0117-311-1462
TICKET DETAILS: 0117-311-1461
CLUBSHOP: 0117-929-8829
WEBSITE: www.bristolrugby.co.uk

responsibility of the rugby club.
Therefore it should be understood that this report is generally about the way a punter would find the ground on a match day.
Many of the above noted criticisms are not the fault of the club and in some cases completely out of their hands.

CAMBRIDGE UNIVERSITY

University Football Ground, Grange Road, Cambridge, CB3 9BN.

ONE of the most civilised experiences in life is to be able to sit in the courtyard of King's College, Cambridge and listen to the beautiful singing voices coming from the main hall. On a cold dark winter's evening, with a touch of frost in the air, the bright lights from the college illuminate the quadrangle, bringing an atmosphere of culture, pleasure and contentment.

On a summer's day a walk along The Backs starting at Magdalene College, by the bridge over the River Cam, is also invigorating for the soul. Wander past St John's, Trinity, Gonville & Caius, Trinity Hall, King's, St Catharine's and Queens', and the aura of academe will have seeped into your system.

Then turn to your right and walk along the few hundred yards which is West Road. At the end, across

Grange Road, is the ground of Cambridge University Rugby Football Club.

The arboreal environment of the area is catching. Although Grange Road is a mixture of large private houses and Halls of Residence the ambience can catch you with the thought of: 'Was this part of the Arcadia of Albion so treasured by previous generations?'

"Oi, guv. Are you coming in then?"

I was snapped out of my romantic illusion by a practical gateman who no doubt thought 'here's a nutter, if ever I saw one' as I was dreamily looking around at the spires and gargoyles on nearby buildings.

As you enter the ground the first thing that hits you is the design of the pavilion. It is like the grand-stands of two centuries ago which dominated racecourses of the time. Upstairs are the club offices where Phil Harvey organises everything which happens in the vicinity. He was generous with his time and dug around the archives for the illus-tration which accompanies this article.

There are two access points but only one is usually open on a match day. They are both in Grange Road and comprise a total of four turnstiles for the paying spectator and a gateway for members. There are car park spaces within the ground but the club also has an arrangement for parking facilities on a site in nearby Old Rifle Range Road, which is just behind the Comber Stand.

As you enter the pavilion, from the doors which face out onto the pitch, the history of the place strikes home, for on the walls are plaques commemorating the University football and rugby teams from 1871 to 2001. The famous names are all there. I counted over one hundred who had gone on to further sporting excellence once their days of study were over. Other spectators came to read the names: they were quiet, for this place is like a sporting shrine.

The Members' Stand, to give it its correct nomenclature, has viewing from two levels with just over one thousand seats, all of which are under cover. Opposite is the Comber Stand which seats 1500, also under shelter, with standing room for another thousand people on the concrete terracing around the rest of the pitch.

The western part of the pavilion is split into two sections. First there is a large bar for the use of both members and general spectators. Along the far wall are various cabinets which contain relics and mementoes of past glories. In the middle of these are double doors which lead to the dining room. This expanse is also for public use and contains the refreshment area.

The selection available is a credit to the chef who was on duty. To start with we were offered three types of home-made soup. I went for the zucchini which was superb: it had been many years since I last sampled this vegetable as a soup. Others in the queue went for further offerings which included hot pies, sandwiches and cakes, none of which were from the conveyor belts of food factories. These were all fresh made products.

While sitting enjoying my suste-nance I took time to read the match programme. It is a standard University effort of 20 pages of which nine were text. However, the amount of information written for us was top rate and the detail given about the night's opponents was really quite good. The programme also noted the fact that replica jerseys were the only items currently available from the club shop.

Walking around the beautifully kept ground is a pleasure. The eastern (Grange Road) side has the groundsman's cottage by the gates and a splendid scoreboard behind the goal. Further back are a row of trees which add to the warmth of the area. The northern part is mainly

CAMBRIDGE UNI. 74%

How Grange Road rates...

Access:	7
Car Parking:	6
Staff Attitude:	8
Comfort & Cleanliness:	9
Programme:	6
Catering:	9
Scenery & Surroundings:	10
Bars:	7
Club Shop:	4
Viewing & Shelter:	8
Total:	74 %
Ranking:	=19th

ADDRESS: University Football Ground, Grange Road, Cambridge, CB3 9BN

DIRECTIONS: From the M11 (Junction 12) and travel along Barton Road for two miles into Cambridge. After a pelican crossing turn left into Grange Road. The ground is situated a mile on the left hand side. Nearest Railway station is Cambridge.

PARKING: At the ground and nearby on Old Rifle Range Road.

TELEPHONE: 01223-354131

FAX: 01223-355301

WEBSITE: www.curufc.com

covered with the Comber Stand, underneath which is a compact gymnasium. I was offered free use of the facilities but I declined with a graceful smile.

As I walked towards the western end I realised that you could hear the roar from the motorway some miles away. It had never crossed my mind that the flatness of the land of this part of Cambridgeshire would allow noise to travel so far.

Behind this part of the ground is a football pitch where a representative match had taken place a couple of hours earlier against the Amateur Football Alliance. As I watched, the portable floodlights were being prepared for a move to an adjacent hockey pitch for a fixture due to be played the next day.

The general comfort and cleanliness was as good as could possibly be expected. The toilet facilities were first class and good provision had been made for disabled people. Although some of the seats were from yesteryear there was no way anyone could complain about the lack of enjoyment a visit to Grange Road always brings.

Barker's Butts Lane, Coundon Road, Coventry, Warwickshire, CV6 1DU.

WHENEVER I go to Coventry there are two city centre places I always try to visit. The De Vere Hotel and the Old Windmill public house. The former is a modern hotel which overlooks the magnificent cathedral and, by walking through a conservatory, you gain access to Cathedral Square. To sit in the courtyard outside the hotel's Daimler Bar, while sipping cappuccino, is one of life's little pleasures.

On the other hand the Old Windmill in Spon Street, a convenient walk away from the Coventry Rugby Football Ground in Coundon Road, is the best real ale pub in the area. Unlike the rest of the buildings in the street, a collection of transplanted survivors from the blitz, this timber-framed fifteenth century ale house is on its original site. Known locally as 'Ma Brown's,' after a former landlady, the pre-match lunches are a speciality.

Contemporary stories look at Coventry as the city in England with the worst devastation resulting from bombing in the last European war, yet it is also an industrial centre. The building of motor vehicles and the production of its ancillary components form the hub of the local economy.

As well, the place has been known by decades of sniggering schoolboys as the home of Lady Godiva whose ninth century naked antics are regularly repeated by moronic spectators who encroach on to modern day football fields. Her statue is to be found in Broadgate which is now the centre of the pedestrianised shopping district.

At the end of the aforementioned Spon Street is a subway which takes you under the Ringway which encircles the city centre. At the end a left turn takes you to Butts Stadium which is being rebuilt as the rugby club's new home.

A right turn sees you in Coundon Road, an inner suburb of large Victorian terrace homes now mostly split into numerous flats or bedsits.

On the right, by a level crossing, is an oasis in the residential wilderness: Bablake School, a private co-educational institution, whose grounds of green expanse and numerous overhanging trees offer a stunning contrast.

Immediately over the train lines, which carry commuters to Nuneaton, on the left is the club's sixty-seven space car parking area which is fenced off from the actual ground. The factory next door, which dominates the view from the main stand, is owned by London Taxis International where the famous black cabs are built.

The eastern side of the ground is actually in Barker's Butts Lane with The Counden public house opposite. Although street parking is ample to meet any needs it is not recommended to park next door to the pub as this is where the Pet Aid Hospital have their accident and emergency centre. Beware of frantic owners parking wildly prior to dashing in to get treatment for their ill or injured animals.

At a first glance the rugby ground looks tatty and a bit of a mess. Look closer and a realisation dawns that much goes on in cramped circumstances.

The northern boundary, stated as being the 'Sheep Pen,' has a permanent wooden structure known as the 'Former Players' Lounge,' as well as a small marquee called the 'Chicken Shack.' This is where a pre-match group dine, naturally, on chicken. When I popped my head around the entrance to see what was going on I was immediately invited to join them. Alas, I had to refuse their kind offer as work always comes first.

The west terrace is mainly covered by a cowshed style of

roofing and can probably accommodate around five thousand spectators. At the rear is a tea bar which seems to do a roaring trade judging by the permanent match day queues.

The southern end has been stripped of much of its terracing in order for rubberised ground sheets to be put in place, presumably for training purposes.

In the south-west corner a large hut called the 'Horses Trough' is actually where the ball-boys have their home. On the walls are honour boards which recall the winners of past youth trophies.

The main stand is quite antiquated and has seating arrangements for 840, all of whom are under cover. The wooden planks are not uncomfortable and the bench style brings back memories of grounds of long ago; Coventry having survived so far. The views are not inspirational although trees behind both goals added some needed greenery to the place.

Right inside the clubhouse door is the Club Shop. There are the usual items of clothing available as well as holdalls, cufflinks, hats and scarves. However, what I did find exciting was that the club have such pride in their county that they had Warwickshire Rugby Football Union embossed clothing for sale. I had not seen this anywhere before and the shop manager assured me

that they sold better, at times, than club material.

The main bar is huge, one of the largest on the rugby circuit. Capable of holding many hundred in comfort, the actual bar runs the full length of the room. At one end was a hot food counter with pies and soup available and, as a treat, hot pork, stuffing and apple rolls as a speciality.

At the far end a door leads into the Pemberton Room which is the members' bar and refreshment area. Here is where a lot of memorabilia is situated but, again, it was the obvious county pride which shone through. One quite superb enlarged photograph showed the Warwickshire and All Blacks teams who met in December 1924. There were also other pictures of this match, and the programme, all preserved for people like me to drool over.

Upstairs were the club offices and sponsors areas where meals were served in rooms whose walls are decorated with illustrations of past glories.

At the far end of the building a large hatchway from the kitchen opened out to provide fans with refreshments. The menu was wide although not out of the ordinary.

The match programme was of thirty-two pages, of which nearly half were advertisements. The 'Club News' section was excellent

COVENTRY 67%

How Coundon Road rates...

Access:	7
Car Parking:	5
Staff Attitude:	8
Comfort & Cleanliness:	6
Programme:	6
Catering:	7
Scenery & Surroundings:	6
Bars:	7
Club Shop:	9
Viewing & Shelter:	6
Total:	67 %
Ranking:	=34th

ADDRESS: Barker's Butts Lane, Coundon, Coventry, Warwickshire, CV6 1DU

DIRECTIONS: From the ring road take the A414 to Birmingham, turn right at traffic lights. Coming into Coventry on the A45 pick up the A414 turn left at the Hollyhead public house, right at the traffic lights and the ground is on the right. The nearest railway station is Coventry.

PARKING: Ample street parking nearby.

TELEPHONE: 024-7660-1174

FAX: 024-7660-1194

WEBSITE: www.coventryrugby.co.uk

although the series of player guides would have been useful had they all been together.

Coventry have been on their present site since 1925 and are looking at one more season before a move. If that is the case, then if you haven't yet visited Coundon Road you know there is not much time left.

Castle Park, Armthorpe Road, Doncaster, South Yorkshire, DN2 5QB.

THE old name for Doncaster was Danum and more than once it was sacked by the invading Danes. The town as we know it came into being in 1194 when it was granted a charter by Richard the Lionhart. With a vast store of coal in the neighbourhood and over five hundred industries, the area, at its peak, was one of the main commercial and manufacturing centres of England.

The town is also known for its race meetings, the first of which was run in 1703. The St Leger was started only a few years later. If you proceed along Leger Way to the end of the racecourse, and turn right towards Armthorpe, you come across a sign which says 'Castle Park.' This is the home of Doncaster Rugby Football Club.

Had you carried on towards Armthorpe a few hundred yards past the entrance is Markham Main Colliery, one of Yorkshire's major pits. A few more yards would find a small church, built by the Normans with fifteenth century windows and a mass dial from the days before clocks.

Within seconds of moving along

the driveway the brand new £2,500,000 clubhouse and conference centre comes into view. Situated in twenty acres of parkland the club has a main ground, with a spectator capacity of 4252, and five further pitches available for either other teams or for community use. The total cost of renovating the whole complex was over one million pounds more, but a Sport England Lottery grant of £1.79 million did help considerably.

Access to the ground is by this one entrance which, incidentally, is opposite Wheatley Golf Club. There is car parking for four hundred vehicles by the clubhouse and for an unlimited number around and behind the main covered stand.

There is seating for 252 in the West Stand as well as standing at the back. The 'Back-of-the-Stand-Gang,' as they are known, are vocal one-eyed supporters whose wit and humour during a match belies their age. A plaque records the official opening by the Mayor back in September 1985.

Towards the south-west corner is what remains of the old clubhouse. Presumably it is used as a store, but what did disappoint me was the mess further on. The carcasses of two rusting road containers and some industrial rubbish spoilt the ambience of the place. Maybe one day they might disappear.

At the southern end of the ground sits the electronic scoreboard before you come to the uncovered concrete terracing on the east side which can accommodate 1772 fans. There are plans to put a

roof over this area which is a splendid idea. The northern end is where the clubhouse is sited.

The view from the stand is over the trees to the bank of the colliery with occasional trains on a freight line passing by. Looking right the trees of Sandall Beat Wood are prominent while the western boundary is dominated by allotment gardens.

The matchday programme is a forty page publication which contains a considerable amount of news. Most impressive was the bold 'Mission Statement,' prominently displayed, which set out what the club were determined to achieve and the time it should take them. When you consider that ten years ago the club were playing in the Yorkshire leagues this is a pretty bold state of mind.

The club shop (actually a couple of tables in the entrance hall) is open after all first team games. The selection was good and sizes of most clothing items went up to and beyond my size, which I always find remarkable. Also on sale were tie clips, cloth badges (but no metal ones much to the angst of a visiting official), glasses, hats and the usual ephemeral items.

The clubhouse is quite a splendid building. If you believe all of the blurb in the impressive printed brochures then any company not using the conference facilities at Castle Park are completely off beam. It is argued that: 'When sporting themes are added to corporate objectives the result is a tremendous increase in memorable positive associations.' It all sounds very good except I haven't a clue what it means.

The ground floor area comprises numerous changing rooms for both male and female players; a splendid first-aid room; multi-purpose gymnasia, offices, a large hallway and stairwell, toilet facilities especially for the disabled and a lift.

The first floor function room catered for 376 people at the lunch I attended. With the close co-operation of local schools most of the serving staff were pupils earning extra pocket-money while also being made aware of the hospitality industry. I was made aware of, and was greatly impressed with, the club's community involvement which is, alas, far too detailed to mention here.

The upstairs suites had the rugby names of Twickenham, Arms Park, Millennium, Lansdowne and Murrayfield, although some of these are parts of a larger room.

The three bars are also on the first floor. One is for general use prior to a game while the others host the lunches. I was told that bar takings in 2001 were £140,000 which rose to £160,000 last year. That is some figure.

DONCASTER 76%

How Castle Park rates...

Access:	8
Car Parking:	8
Staff Attitude:	9
Comfort & Cleanliness:	7
Programme:	8
Catering:	9
Scenery & Surroundings:	7
Bars:	6
Club Shop:	7
Viewing & Shelter:	7
Total:	76 %
Ranking:	=16th

ADDRESS: Castle Park, Armthorpe Road, Doncaster, South Yorkshire, DN2 5QB

DIRECTIONS: Leave M18 (Junction 4) and follow the A630 towards Doncaster. Turn left at the second roundabout into Armthorpe and right at the mini-roundabout in Armthorpe. The ground is one mile on the left.
The nearest Railway Stations are Doncaster or Kirk Sandal (Two and a quarter miles from the ground).

PARKING: Unlimited parking available.

TELEPHONE: 01302-831388

FAX: 01302-831496

WEBSITE: www.drfc.co.uk

In all the glory of its near perfect building there were two things which bothered me. The first was the appalling overcrowding of the main bar area after the game. It was a fight to get in the door as some 450 people stood around drinking. I then battled my way to the serving hatch to get some food but had to battle back as the intense smoke from cigarettes nearly brought on an asthma attack. In any case had I found anyone I knew we could only have made signs at each other for the loud music made shouting the only possible method of communication.

With regret I have to say that I was very pleased to get out of the chaos of the room.

The other gripe concerned catering: not the superb meal I thoroughly enjoyed but from the point of view of a matchday punter. At half time I looked around for a hot drink but where could I get one? I went without. Even now I don't know if there was anywhere to purchase them.

However, for all of my various comments one thing remains: there is a serious problem for any rugby visitor to Castle Park. The hospitality is so infectious and the atmosphere so warm that the game can feel totally superfluous to the kindness on offer.

Meadowbank Stadium, London Road, Edinburgh, EH7 6AE.

THIRTY-SIX years ago at a meeting held in Kingston, Jamaica the 1970 Commonwealth Games were awarded to the city of Edinburgh. Within a few weeks of that April meeting an organising committee had been formed in Scotland and, by February 1967, Edinburgh Corporation had started to renovate the Meadowbank Sports Centre.

Originally built in 1960 with a grant from the Sports Council, the Corporation set about bringing the Stadium up to the then internationally accepted standard of 15,000 permanent seats. Added to this were temporary seating arrangements to double the capacity for the duration of the event. This was also the case for the 1986 Games.

In 1975 the Scottish Football League decided to restructure their divisions and they elected a works team, Ferranti Thistle, to even up the numbers. The club immediately arranged to base themselves at the then unused stadium and changed their name to Meadowbank Thistle.

The team made very little impact on Scottish football until a controversial Edinburgh builder took over as chairman. His blunt attitude alienated the small fan base and the decision to relocate to the new town of Livingston in 1997 caused a furore. A change of name and a new home, the newly constructed Almondvale Stadium, meant that the name Meadowbank was lost to football fans. It is ironic that plans are now at an advanced stage to move the rest of the Meadowbank sports complex to a site next to the Livingston ground.

The determination of the Scottish Rugby Football Union some years ago to form professional teams, with one being based in Edinburgh, raised the possibility that Meadowbank Stadium might be used for some of their matches. However it was not until near the end of last season, when there were problems using the Myreside ground, that the decision was taken to play at the stadium.

The area known as Meadowbank is situated a mile east of the city centre and has Holyrood Park as its southern boundary. Access to the stadium is easy from all directions with the incredibly tall floodlight pylons acting as beacons for miles around. A car park capable of taking 480 vehicles has its poorly marked entrance from the main London Road. However, once it is full street parking becomes difficult, as Edinburgh is a city of few spaces and zealous traffic wardens.

There are no signs to direct a stranger to the sports field and twice I ended up entering a wrong part of the complex. Finally the right admission point was found but before going in I visited the club caravan. There was very little on sale: mainly shirts in club colours and colour photographs of the players. In a corner was the media accreditation desk (which the club's public relations company had previously denied existed) and within a few minutes I was the proud owner of 'Media Pass #1.'

There were four turnstiles in use for the match and they were all at the back of the main South Stand. I found the Chief Steward, explained who I was and what I was doing, then asked him if he could tell me how many turnstiles there were.

"I'm not telling you," was his reply. It's a secret: a Health and Safety security requirement and, anyway, I don't talk to the press."

On my return from walking around the stadium I met him again.

"You've got twenty-eight turnstiles," I whispered to him. "But I won't tell anybody."

He glared at me. So I went for broke: "You couldn't tell me the capacity of the ground or that of the main stand, could you?" I gave him one of my winsome smiles but it didn't work.

"I'm not telling you anything. It's

a classified figure." he replied. The three other stewards around him nodded knowingly. I walked less than twenty feet from them, went through a swing door into the walkway which led to the pressbox and, lo and behold, a noticeboard on the wall had a large map of the stadium. It was a safety announcement, which told me that the main stand area seated 6100 spectators with the rest of the uncovered areas accommodating 7700. Twenty minutes later I saw him again. "It's 13,800," I said out of the side of my mouth. He pursed his lips and looked upwards. It was time to go.

What I had also found out was that only the main stand could be used for rugby which, in effect, meant that only 6100 fans could be admitted. As the stadium was over thirty years old Edinburgh Leisure (a Corporation department) were reluctant to grant a usage certificate for the outer areas without much needed renovation having first been completed.

On my way to get a hot drink I looked around for a programme seller. There were none to be seen so I asked at the ticket entrance. "There are no programmes today," said the person on duty.

I asked the obvious question. "How will the spectators know who is playing?"

"They can listen to Jimmy on the tannoy. He reads out who is in the teams."

This was getting all too much. I needed coffee, but where were the refreshment stalls? Stalls? Actually it was a trestle table, which held two urns, piles of polystyrene cups, a jar of powdered coffee, tea bags, sugar and a selection of two types of chocolate wafers. Twenty feet to the left was a hatchway with a banner stating 'Hot Pies.' I bought one: it was stone cold. And this was to service a matchday crowd of 4500!

The beer area was not much better. Situated at the far end of the entrance hall, away from the turnstiles, an obviously temporary bar staffed by five youngsters serviced less than eighty patrons. Admittedly a far superior bar was in use within the sports complex for corporate hospitality guests but this was out of bounds to the normal everyday fan.

Once in the stand the view of the playing area - looking over the equivalent of twenty lanes of the running track - was so distant that at times, when the players were furthest away from the spectators, it was impossible to know which side was which.

Losing concentration during the match was a common occurrence but to make up for it the scenery and surroundings were most pleasant. As the giant electronic scoreboard had given up the ghost

EDINBURGH 37%

How Meadowbank Stadium rates...

Access:	4
Car Parking:	6
Staff Attitude:	1
Comfort & Cleanliness:	6
Programme:	0
Catering:	2
Scenery & Surroundings:	6
Bars:	4
Club Shop:	4
Viewing & Shelter:	4

Total:	37 %
Ranking:	50th

ADDRESS: Meadowbank Stadium, London Road, Edinburgh, EH7 6AE

DIRECTIONS: From the South - Meadowbank lies on the A1 and is easily accessible. From the North - From Forth Road Bridge join A720, Edinburgh by-pass to A7 junction, continue as above.
From the west you can travel east along Glasgow Road, through Corstorphine and Roseburn to Queen Street then continue as above.
Nearest Railway Station is Edinburgh.

PARKING: 480 spaces are available, entrance from London Road.

TELEPHONE: Stadium: 0131-661-5351

TICKET DETAILS: 0845-456-0017

WEBSITE:
www.sru.org.uk/proteam/edinburgh

half an hour before the start, I was lucky to find myself seated next the local statistician who gave me immeasurable assistance.

Had I been a paying punter at the match I would have been both shocked and saddened at the whole atmosphere and attitude of the place. It is not a rugby ground and never will be. A return to Myreside would be wonderful.

Molesey Road, Hersham, Surrey, KT12 3PF.

WATER, water everywhere. That is what you might say when visiting the Molesey Road ground of Esher Rugby Football Club. Wherever you go in the immediate vicinity there is water: the enormous Queen Elizabeth II Reservoir is situated immediately to the north of the ground and behind that are loads of other water storage holding areas.

To the east, ignoring the flooded gravel pits, is the Island Barn Reservoir while in front is the meeting place of the Rivers Mole and Ember. Westwards is the River Thames and flowing towards the ground is the not so well known River Engine. There are boat marinas all over the place, especially a mile away at Shepperton.

To add to the local delights, the oil terminal opposite Wheatley's Ait is just south of the gasworks, while three urban farms are wrapped around the QE2 waterworks.

Farms abound in this part of Hersham, although most of them have lost land to 'Industrial Parks' and 'Trading Estates.' The

Metropolitan Police Dog Training Centre is opposite the ground to the east behind various three-storey office blocks, while behind that is Sandown Park Racecourse. Talking of racing, Kempton Park Racecourse is due north and how many of you can remember its famous old neighbour, Hurst Park Racecourse, now long gone?

The train service from Waterloo is excellent by today's standards and takes just half an hour. Opposite Hersham Station is a greasy-spoon cafe: If you suffer from cardiovascular problems or are on a strict diet then walk past with your nose in the air and mannerisms of I-wouldn't-go-in-there-even-if-you-paid-me. If not, then dive inside and try any one of Mick's all-day specialities.

The property along Molesey Road varies from fairly good to better than ordinary. A cluster of new medium-density detached houses are in a Close immediately to the south of the Club but the design is such that only a couple overlook the ground and light spillage from the floodlights is not a problem.

There have been many changes at the Club in the past two years, more in fact since they moved to the present site in 1937. Formed in 1923, by the time of the outbreak of war, eight sides were playing on a regular basis. By the early 1950s there were fifteen competing teams, following a huge influx of players. Twenty years later the Club could afford to purchase outright its twenty-seven acre ground and to build a new stand. They claim to have been the first rugby club in London to erect floodlights, although I have no proof one way or the other.

Access is from the main road and is easy to find. A large board advertises future games and welcomes new visitors. Immediately inside, on the left, are marked spaces for cars and coaches. To the right, parallel to the road, is the site of the recent portakabin changing rooms and various marquees. Now the new clubhouse is open for business, the majority of this area has been tarmacked and white-lined for parking vehicles. I counted 320 spaces with a further 240 available on gravel and grass further on.

Behind the northern goal and western stand are the other seven pitches which, by the look of them, are used on a very regular basis. Also, the division between them and the main pitch is marked by two long rows of poplar trees which stand tall like sentries guarding their barracks. My visit was for a night match in early spring and the noise from mating birds was a cacophony of screeching. If you visit while this is in progress, a word of warning: don't stand under the trees.

The peace is also shattered by planes taking off from nearby Heathrow Airport and trains running along a high embankment. The land here is very flat and it was obvious that the water-table is not too far below the surface. A stagnant brook divided the first and second team pitches and at the rear were a miscellany of post-war dwellings looking like a patchwork quilt with the designs of different decades.

More noise came from the generator sited at the northern end of the main stand. It serviced the busy mobile phone mast which looked like a leftover from the novel 'War of the Worlds' which was based in this area. Although having wooden benches, the 998 seater stand was comfortable and had excellent viewing. Even with spectators to my side and in front, all parts of the pitch could be seen easily.

The clubhouse takes up most of the southern part of the complex and was opened for business in January 2001. Grant aided by the Foundation for Sport and the Arts the building has two large bar and dining areas. The main function room can seat 264 for dinner in very comfortable circumstances. There are snippets of memorabilia decorating the walls, but the main items are to be found in the adjoining public bar.

It is quite probable that up to four hundred people could drink in comfort in this room which also provides hot drinks and snacks. For cold winter days the old fashioned fireplace comes into use, although I

ESHER   66%

How Molesey Road rates...

Access:	7
Car Parking:	8
Staff Attitude:	7
Comfort & Cleanliness:	7
Programme:	6
Catering:	5
Scenery & Surroundings:	6
Bars:	7
Club Shop:	6
Viewing & Shelter:	7
Total:	66 %
Ranking:	=36th

ADDRESS: Molesey Road, Hersham, Surrey, KT12 3PF

DIRECTIONS: Leave M25 (Junction 10) onto A3 towards London. After 1 mile turn left to Walton-on-Thames (A245). After 1/4 mile turn right at traffic lights into Seven Hills Road (B365). Turn right at small roundabout into Burwood Road and follow this into Hersham Village, bearing right into Molesey Road. Keep straight on at large roundabout, under railway bridge at Hersham Station and the ground is 300 yards on the left.
From central London take the A3 out of London and continue down to turn-off to Esher (A244). Follow this road (Copsem Lane/Claremont Lane) through Esher Village, and across High Street into Church Street, turn left into Lammas Lane towards Walton-on-Thames (A244) along dual carriageway. Turn right at large round-about into Molesey Road, under the railway bridge at Hersham Station, and the ground is 300 yards on the left.
The nearest Railway Station is Hersham.

PARKING: 560 spaces available at the ground.

TELEPHONE: 01932-220295

CLUBHOUSE: 01932-224834

FAX: 01932-254627

WEBSITE: www.esherrfc.org

have no idea if Hersham is in a smokeless zone. On match days a burger van plonks itself in the car park but otherwise it's filled rolls and pasties at the bar.

Just by the doors which separate the two rooms is a splendidly-designed club shop. It has wooden shutters for the counter and is very user friendly. On sale are the usual range of embossed clothing such as tops, t-shirts, polo sweaters and shirts along with scarves, badges, sox and hats.

The western part of the building also has a 'Psysiotherapy (sic) Clinic' as well as the changing rooms. This former area turns itself into a sponsor's lounge on match days.

The match programme is a forty-eight page glossy publication of which thirty-six are pre-prepared. Like most modern day issues this carries excellent details and photographs of the players which, for a first time visitor, are extremely helpful.

Although the club is active in all tiers of the game and provides committeemen at the highest level, I could not help wondering if something was missing. What it is, I can't say but I just was left with that feeling.

Hughenden Road, Glasgow, G12 9XP.

SOMETHING which has bothered me for a while is the perception of Glasgow by people living south of the border. They seem to denigrate the place, yet it has a breadth and depth of outstanding culture. In fact it was not that long ago that Glasgow spent a year with the moniker 'Cultural City of Europe.'

From a sporting point of view the Scottish Football Association Museum at Hampden Park is, without question, the most splendid of its type in the world. In other sports there are fine stadia with good facilities, particularly for rugby, athletics, bowls, shinty, football, cricket and tennis.

So often Scotland, and Scottish sport, are decried by the London-based white-wine-dining sub-intellectuals who have caused havoc over the years with their influential ignorance of sport around the globe. They gauge their Scottish oblivi-ousness purely upon the religious bigotry of two soccer clubs.

Whenever I am in Strathclyde I

base myself eight miles from the city centre in a spot near to the River Clyde and Bothwell Castle. The suburbs are quiet and inviting. The drive to the centre of Glasgow is all done by motorway in a few minutes.

To get to the Hughenden ground is just a matter of joining the Great Western Road and going through the University-dominated suburbs of Kelvinbridge and Dowanhill until the Hillhead Sports Club beckons. The area is called Hyndland and is rumoured to be the creme-de-la-creme of Glasgow's inner suburbs. If the quality of the property in streets around the ground is anything to go by then the rumour must be fact.

The sporting complex is the home of Hillhead squash, hockey, cricket, rugby and tennis clubs as well as the Glasgow Mid Argyle Shinty Club. The extensive grounds stretch for some distance away from the rugby pitch and must be worth millions of pounds in the eyes of a property developer.

Street parking in the area is easy with spaces plentiful. From wherever you leave your vehicle the walk will always bring you to Hughenden Road and the two entrance points at each extremity of the eastern part of the ground. Once inside there is immediate temptation, for along the terrace is a large mobile catering van which sells a dozen varieties of coffee with large doughnuts and even larger muffins as optional extras. Cappuccino a-la Hughenden is not to be missed.

The main stand on the southern side takes 815 sitting spectators, with the western stand another 630. There is terracing for over four thousand of which about a third would be under cover.

As I meandered around, the stewards were chatty and helpful. One of them pointed out the novel lighting which illuminates the scoreboard in the south-west corner while another showed me around the kitchen areas. Outside catering was provided by two commercial burger outlets and one run by club volunteers (whose offerings were twice the size and half the price).

A large marquee, to the right of the clubhouse, provided beers and spirits for the general spectators. I was told that fifteen hundred people could be accommodated in comfort. On the night of my visit the after-match singing, by visiting victorious Welsh fans, was still going strong an hour after the final whistle had been blown.

The clubhouse was a grand two-storey building which spread over a wide area. Downstairs was reserved purely for changing rooms and storage space while upstairs had a large function room with bar, two members' bars, boardroom,

kitchens, cloakrooms and a seeming maze of corridors.

Although the Hillhead and Jordanhill clubs had amalgamated in 1988, the large amount of memorabilia around the place was mainly of the latter. Glasgow is too new a club to have anything yet worth recording. What was on display comprised old international shirts, large wooden tablets recording the names of past worthies, numerous plaques on the walls and a designated `Bruce Borland Memorial' display case.

In the boardroom the walls were festooned with portrait photographs of Olympians and champions of the Sports Club. As well as sports previously mentioned, there were Scottish swimming, badminton, athletic and golf winners, all of whom had been members in one shape or form.

The main negative was the club shop which constituted a few pieces of clothing on a solitary rack in the centre of a so-called 'Exhibition Visit Hire' van. No one present wanted to talk about the lack of items available and it was clear that there was a problem somewhere along the line.

The matchday programme was a standard effort of forty-eight pages of which nineteen were advertising. However thirteen of these pages were rugby related adverts which left an impression of more editorial than was actually the case.

Sitting in the pressbox at the top of the main stand was a delight. As I looked right, there was a row of

GLASGOW 70%

How Hughenden rates...

Access:	6
Car Parking:	6
Staff Attitude:	9
Comfort & Cleanliness:	7
Programme:	7
Catering:	7
Scenery & Surroundings:	9
Bars:	8
Club Shop:	3
Viewing & Shelter:	8
Total:	70 %
Ranking:	=27th

ADDRESS: Hughenden Road, Glasgow, G12 9XP.

DIRECTIONS: From the north or east, exit the M8 (Junction 17) signposted Dumbarton. At the end of the slip road, turn right and take the fly-over back across the motorway. Follow this road (Great Western Road) for around 3km, pass the Botanic Gardens on your right and go straight through the next set of traffic lights. Turn left at the following set of traffic lights into Hyndland Road, then first right after the tennis club.
From the south or west, exit the M8 (Junction 18) signposted Dumbarton. Follow this road (Great Western Road) as per the directions above.
Nearest Railway Stations are Hillhead (Underground from Buchanan Street or St Enoch) or Hyndland by low level train.

PARKING: On-street parking available nearby.

TELEPHONE: 0141-353-3468

CLUBHOUSE: 0141-357-1115

FAX: 0141-332-5875

TICKET DETAILS: 0845-6060268

WEBSITE:
www.sru.org.uk/proteam/glasgow

five-storey Victorian terraced houses all along the other side of Hughenden Road. Many had their curtains open and lights blazed through, so giving a view of rooms with high ceilings, most of which seemed tastefully decorated. Many of the occupants were watching the night's proceedings through the leafless trees which were strung along the back of the terracing.

To my left across the playing fields was the constant traffic of the main road. Behind me were new apartment buildings, the cost of which brought shudders from fellow journalists. The whole area oozed class and quality: it is that sort of place.

(N.B. This is also the home ground of Hillhead/Jordanhill RFC who play in Scottish Premiership Division Three)

Kingsholm, Kingsholm Road, Gloucester, GL1 3AX.

THE city of Gloucester has always been a puzzle to me. Some of it is historical, cultured and appealing, while other parts are places which send a shiver of foreboding down your spine.

Not so many years ago a terrible series of crimes took place in Cromwell Street which is so central to the town that its rear is by the back of the Museum, Library and Art Gallery. Wearing my hat as an investigative reporter of old, I walked the streets around this area and just cannot believe that permanent residents and temporary inhabitants of the myriad of short-term leasehold bed-sitting rooms had no idea what was taking place yards from them.

A dichotomy also seems to exist in the central shopping area. There, a mixture of county gentry and urban country bumpkins seem to co-exist more by necessity than by choice. In some ways a helplessness appears to exist amongst the blue-collar element whose open attitude seems to be one of survival more than of consolidation.

The divide opens wide to the west of the city. The cultural redevelopment of the docks area around the basin of the Gloucester & Sharpness Canal is quite superb. Here we have museums, craft centres and a marina, all attracting the tourist dollar. Around the back, by the Gloucester City Football Ground, are wasteland acres used as a Council refuse tip and being scavenged by those in need of

conducting themselves in this way. In winter the gannets hover overhead in packs waiting to strike: in summer an essential item would be a can of insect repellent to ward off the fleas and mosquitoes.

The rugby ground is a few hundred yards north of the city centre in Kingsholm Road. Carry on a mile further and the east opens out to become playing fields and new residential suburbs. To the west is the broad flood plain of the River Severn. Opposite the ground, in the area of Kingsholm, are old terraced homes unlikely to have been

occupied by those sitting in the Grandstand or standing in The Shed. Gloucester supporters do not live on housing benefits: quite the opposite.

By the main entrance is a car park available only to those with the appropriate passes. Otherwise it is on-street parking which, I must confess, I have never found to be a problem. There are four entrance points, one at each corner, with the most popular being those on Worcester Road.

Just inside the car park is the Club Shop. Although it is nowhere near to being as large as other rugby outlets, the quality and variation of the goods available is top rate. The club also do the obvious in giving over two pages of the programme to publicising their products. The range is good, varying from fleeces to flags, calendars to shirts, replica balls to caps. And all at affordable prices. There is also a kiosk inside the ground which sells small items.

The Worcester Road Stand has an allocation of seats, red in colour, which are known as 'community seats.' These are for use by school-children who, by arrangement, come in school parties for allocated matches. The club greatly reduce the ticket prices for these groups. It is a splendid initiative which will surely reap long term benefit.

The southern side of the ground starts with the clubhouse and a vestibule of select memorabilia. The main item is the memorial of the First War which shows that the club lost eighteen players in that appalling waste of humankind. Then the Grandstand, which seats eleven hundred, occupies the middle section, followed by a series of sponsors' boxes.

Behind the west goal is a new hospitality stand, in front of which is terracing under cover for 2600 spectators. The club gave me carte blanche for this article to visit areas usually not accessible to the ordinary punter. So I was able to look closely at what was on offer and my opinion of these suites, which hold a total of 250 people, and of the food being served, could not get a higher rating. As I left, my instinct made me walk behind the building. I turned around and facing me was the glorious building of Gloucester Cathedral. It was a view of absolute stunning beauty.

'The Shed' is known to all rugby fans. With 4250 voices giving an opinion, an opposing player might feel slightly intimidated. A monthly fanzine, 'Shedhead,' is available only to those who stand on its terracing. The view of the Cathedral has been blocked by the sponsors' boxes but the nearby church of St Mark's still gives an ecclesiastical aura to the place.

There were bars and food outlets all around the ground. Some bars

GLOUCESTER 77%

How Kingsholm rates...

Access:	8
Car Parking:	5
Staff Attitude:	9
Comfort & Cleanliness:	8
Programme:	8
Catering:	8
Scenery & Surroundings:	8
Bars:	7
Club Shop:	8
Viewing & Shelter:	8
Total:	77 %
Ranking:	=14th

ADDRESS: Kingsholm, Kingsholm Road, Gloucester, GL1 3AX

DIRECTIONS: Leave the M5 (Junction 11) and follow signs for Gloucester, A40. Follow the dual carriageway to round-about, turn right following A40 signs to Gloucester/Ross on Wye. Follow the dual carriageway to the next roundabout (Longford Roundabout), and turn left following A38 signs to Gloucester City Centre. You come to another roundabout (Tewkesbury Road Roundabout), go straight across following signs to Gloucester City Centre; you are now on the Kingsholm Road, the ground is approx. 800 yards on the right.
From the West use the A48 or A40 into Gloucester. On approaching Gloucester use the A40 Gloucester Northern Bypass. You will then come to the Longford Roundabout and take directions as listed above.
Nearest Railway Station is Gloucester which is less than a 10 minute walk from Gloucester Rugby Club.

PARKING: Two secure car parking facilities are available, otherwise plenty of on-street parking.

TELEPHONE: 0871-871-8781
FAX: 01452-383321

TICKET DETAILS: 0871-871-8781

WEBSITE: www.gloucesterrugbyclub.com

were in the open but under cover and it takes a brave person to down pints on a day as cold as on my visit.

The programme is of sixty-four pages with only a quarter of them being irrelevant advertising. It is a well-produced publication with reliable, interesting articles.

Gloucester is a good old-style rugby club with deeply loyal supporters. Many travel some distance to attend matches and their enthusiasm rubs off on all and sundry.

Ovenden Park, Keighley Road, Halifax, West Yorkshire, HX2 8AR.

WHEN I was just a wisp of a lad my old geography teacher once took his class to listen in to a government inquiry. His intention was to show us how the process worked. The subject under discussion was the building of the south-eastern section of a motorway now known and loved by us all: the M25.

I distinctly remember the submissions that day mainly because, even then, they sounded so absurd to young teenage ears. "This motorway does not need three lanes," burbled the Sevenoaks District Council's planning officer. "In fact, does it even need two?"

This memory often comes back to me when I visit areas developed in the latter half of the last century which are now the root causes of so many social ills. In those days numerous housing and community developments earned their planners medals or even knighthoods. Cynically, in hindsight, one could argue more for a hangman's noose.

One rugby club who have suffered more than most is Halifax, based at the Standeven Memorial Ground in Ovenden Park. While West Yorkshire badly needed new council homes at the time it is, alas, the younger element of succeeding generations who have made their estates into 'no-go' areas of vandalism, graffiti and incomprehensible destruction. Fuelled on high sugar content McMuck style food and unable to relate to their community, these low intelligent beings feel it necessary to trash buildings and vehicles "for a laugh."

How sad it is to enter the well designed clubhouse at Halifax to be confronted by a sign which warns members never to leave their car at the club overnight. Any night.

However, it appears that the local vandals, whose crimefile currently records in excess of sixty separate incidents, have won. The club, whose one thousand seater stand was torched amongst other fires started at the ground, have now decided to sell up and move to a new location on the south side of town where life is more civilised.

In his programme notes, secretary Mike Smith explains: "While we apologise for the actual fabric of Ovenden Park, we do not apologise for our hospitality and the warmth of our welcome to visitors from far and wide." The latter I was soon to experience.

Assessing the ground in its current state I feel it essential to comment that it is in far better repair than some, even from divisions above National Three North where Halifax currently reside.

The only access is from a driveway off Keighley Road which leads down to the club's gates and the first of many car parking areas. To the right is the clubhouse while further down the track are allocated parking places. In wandering around and chatting to club members it seems that the spaces are more than would ever be needed.

On entering the ground the first steward I met greeted me with a "good afternoon." The second directed me towards the clubhouse while the third steward, looking after the entry door said: "Get yourself comfortable and I'll come and get you a pint." My look of absolute shock at this totally unexpected kindness was noted. "Well," he said, "I can tell you are a guest by your accent."

I was flabbergasted. I had to sit down. In all my years on the football circuit and now on the rugby union roundabout I had never had a steward talk to me in this way. Abusive, churlish, dogmatic, petty: yes, times too numerous to mention. But this? Never before. Please let it happen again.

What is left of the repaired main stand now has seventy-five seats. It faces due east across a steep valley to Pule Hill. The escarpment is a painter's dream for I counted over a dozen differing shades of green in the landscape. In the foreground are farm buildings daubed, alas, with indecipherable graffiti.

Behind the southern goal is stone terracing then an earth mound. On the join of the two is the invisible postal boundary between HX2 and HX3. It's amazing the useless information you can relate when compiling these ground reports.

The eastern stand is purely for the shelter of standing spectators with the rest of the area surrounding the pitch being grass

banking. The floodlights were more than adequate as were all walkways.

On entering the clubhouse a left turn will take you into the ample sized bar area. Carry on and a door leads in one direction to the players' changing rooms and in the other to the squash courts. On the wall of the spectator balcony are various honour boards with the names Mallard, Mann and Reynolds dominating over all competitions.

Had you turned right when going inside, the large dining and social room opens up. On the day of my visit lunch for over one hundred sponsors and their guests was easily being accommodated. Another part of the room was used for general dining while the club shop had set up a stall along part of one long wall. The selection of items was excellent and included replica shirts, polo jumpers, bobble hats,

HALIFAX 71%

How Ovenden Park rates...

Access:	6
Car Parking:	7
Staff Attitude:	10
Comfort & Cleanliness:	7
Programme:	8
Catering:	6
Scenery & Surroundings:	7
Bars:	6
Club Shop:	8
Viewing & Shelter:	6
Total:	71 %
Ranking:	=24th

ADDRESS: Ovenden Park, Keighley Road, Halifax, West Yorkshire, HX2 8AR

DIRECTIONS: From Halifax town centre take the main A629 road signposted Keighley. The ground is approx. 2.5 miles from the town centre on the right behind Moorside Junior school. The entry road is just past the school and before Moorside Garage.

PARKING: 500 spaces within the ground.

TELEPHONE: 01422-365926

WEBSITE: www.halifaxrufc.co.uk

scarves, rosettes, mugs, embossed knickers, boxer shorts and toy bears wearing club colours.

I read the programme as I sat and drank coffee having, I must confess, passed over the opportunity to sample any of the fine food on offer. The sixty-eight page publication was an excellent effort and told me everything I needed to know about the club and the day's opponents.

Wherever Halifax do finally put down new roots, having been at Ovenden Park since 1925, we can only wish them better fortune than they have experienced in recent times.

(The club's new ground near to the M62 should be ready for the 2005/06 season.)

The Stoop Memorial Ground, Langhorn Drive, Twickenham, TW2 7SX.

UNTIL 1965, and local government reorganisation, the Urban District Council of Twickenham sat quietly in the county of Middlesex. The land was fertile, as it should be being so near to a huge meander in the River Thames, and for many years market gardens dominated the area. The residents were, in the main, well-to-do from the middle-classes who resided in a dormitory suburb.

Then came two changing factors: the creation of the London Borough of Richmond-upon-Thames and an influx of nouveau-riche bourgeoisie residents with more money than class.

At first little happened to cause any friction between the main sporting clubs in the enlarged Borough until the Rugby Football Union decided to upgrade, then rebuild, their stadium. The saga of the RFU, the local authority and unco-operative residents is not for this article. However, the knock-on effect nearly caused very serious

problems for Harlequins Rugby Football Club, who occupy a site on the other side of Chertsey Road.

Attempts to use The Stoop as a joint rugby union undertaking (first with London Scottish, then London Irish) and rugby league venue (London Broncos) have all failed. The interference and belligerence of both the Council and residents has been a story of unbelievable demands, claims and pettiness. At the present time there is a lull in the battle.

When Adrian Stoop and others chose the land upon which the ground now sits they were looking at flat land with Hounslow Heath to the east, Fulwell Park to the south and Old Deer Park just up the main road. At the time, nearly a century ago, the area would have been a perfect place to site a rugby club.

The development of mass mid-wars housing within the vicinity, which are now the prized expensive possessions of vocal residents, has meant that any proposed changes at The Stoop brings forth howls of outrage and opposition.

Having said that, the improvements made at the ground over the past few years are first class. Walking from Twickenham town centre along Craneford Way, The Stoop comes into view when you see the back of the new 3600 seat East Stand. This complex of spectator seats, sixteen executive boxes, superb dining areas and equivalent bars was erected in double quick time six years ago.

At both ends behind the goals permanent-temporary seating has been erected on scaffolding and here some 5750 spectators can watch in relative comfort, so long as it is not raining. Previous similar structures, of a better design, particularly at the northern end and north-east side, were dismantled due to resident's complaints and council leaders (who were grovelling after cheap votes in a politically evenly divided Borough) taking their side.

The old, West Stand, has 448 seats under cover but it also contains the Harlequins' offices on the first floor and a large bar area at the top. To the right of this structure used to be further seating but I won't repeat the monotonous story as to why this area is now occupied by a marquee which is used as a match day creche.

Access to the ground is from the main Chertsey Road by car or from three other points which have only pedestrian approaches. Car parking is available at various spots around the outside of the perimeter fence and I gather that over 600 vehicles can be parked with ease. There are sixteen turnstiles, various entrances to private boxes and a press gate situated, after it rains, by the largest puddle around. The busy ticket office, located in a large portakabin, is by the north-west gate.

In trying to find details about the ground certain stewards were distinctly unhelpful. Luckily I had known the Safety Officer for some time and he went out of his way to provide me with all the particulars I needed.

Catering at The Stoop is top class. There is everything you could ever want stretching from pre-booked carvery lunches through to a sit-down dining area for hot meals, all of which are available under the new stand. Outside the variation goes from baked potatoes with a dozen choices of extras through to a doughnuts and cappuccino servery.

You are spoilt for choice when it comes to bars. Other than those already mentioned there is the Jester Bar for debenture holders, the Colours Bar for the lunch clientele and the Kings Bar for the general punter. After the game I attended this bar had, on its stage, a well-known band who gave some forceful renditions of their 1980s hit songs.

The community spirit engendered at The Stoop comes through loud and clear by both reading the excellent programme, edited by Nick Melton, and seeing the enthusiasm of all playing groups be they children, women or veterans.

Naturally at Harlequins you do not have a club shop: you have a Merchandise Outlet. In fact there are

HARLEQUINS 78%

How The Stoop rates...

Access:	8
Car Parking:	7
Staff Attitude:	6
Comfort & Cleanliness:	7
Programme:	9
Catering:	10
Scenery & Surroundings:	6
Bars:	9
Club Shop:	8
Viewing & Shelter:	8
Total:	78 %
Ranking:	=11th

ADDRESS: The Stoop Memorial Ground, Langhorn Drive, Twickenham, TW2 7SX

DIRECTIONS: Follow the M3 until it ends at the Sunbury roundabout, continue up the A316 Chertsey Road, over three round-abouts (for approx. 2 miles). With Twickenham Rugby Stadium on your left, Quins' ground is on the right, continue and perform a U-turn at the RFU round-about. Enter the Stoop via Langhorn Drive, 450 yards on your left.
From the M4 or M25: Leave the M4 (Junction 3) and take the third exit of the roundabout for the A312, towards Feltham. Continue along the A312 for 4.5 miles and at the A305/A316 roundabout, turn left onto the A316. Follow the A316 Chertsey Road directions as above. The nearest Railway Station is Twickenham.

PARKING: 600 spaces - available at various spots around the outside of the perimeter fence.

TELEPHONE: 020-8410-6000

FAX: 020-8410-6001

CLUB SHOP: 020-8410-6056

WEBSITE: www.quins.co.uk

three of them, all situated on the eastern side of the ground. Had you come through nearby Richmond to the match you would have seen the club's shop: If through Twickenham town centre, the new superstore. However, don't go looking for cheap bargains. This is Harlequins country.

The sixty-four page programme is a life-and-times story of the club. The advertised events planned are mouth-watering. My pick was the 'City Dinner,' a black tie event, a snip of an evening for you and the lads at £1150 (plus VAT). The programme also has an eight-page supplement for younger supporters which is a splendid concept.

The immediate scenery and surroundings do not live up to the high expectations when you get inside the ground. To the south is a council depot where trundling waste vans make their presence known. To the east is Richmond-Upon-Thames College; swing round to a health club and directly north is rugby's massive headquarters. Look upwards and you see you are directly underneath the main flightpath into Heathrow Airport. It's never quiet at The Stoop.

County Ground, Claro Road, Harrogate, North Yorkshire, HG1 4AG.

THE roads leading into Harrogate always seem to be crowded. Whether it be winter shoppers or summer tourists all thoroughfares to the centre of this spa of eighty natural springs are chock full of crawling vehicles.

This comes as a surprise after travelling through the quiet Dales of North Yorkshire and arriving in this splendid town sited to the immediate south of the River Nidd. There is so much on offer in Harrogate, be it Betty's Tea Rooms (the made-on-the-premises chocolate is devastating) through to looking at the superb architecture of the theatre and Grand Opera House.

In fact there are many interesting places within the area of the town centre which are worthy of visiting before a match at Claro Road, home of Harrogate Rugby Football Club. The ground is at the eastern end of a huge swathe of parkland known as 'The Stray' (part of the old Forest of Knaresborough) and about five minutes walk from the shopping district.

Harrogate is known for its conferences, especially the political ones, and they take place in the Royal Hall another of the splendid Victorian buildings which dominate the skyline. It is an ideal venue situated as it is exactly halfway between the capitals of England and Scotland.

The town has a fine group of churches and chapels, the best by far being Christ Church which is opposite Claro Road on the Stray. Built in 1831 it has rich glass at its east end and had early connections with the rugby club in the latter stages of the Victorian era and through Edwardian times.

It was in this church in 1919 that the club honoured its twenty-three players lost in the war, a scene repeated in 1946 when homage was paid to another departed twelve.

The main entrance to the ground is through a gate about two hundred yards along Claro Road from The Stray. There is another access point further back but this is for spectators only. Once inside there is ample parking room as the club occupies eleven and a half acres of prime land. I counted at least three hundred spaces on gravel with many more available on grass.

The clubhouse and main pitch are in the north-west of the complex, with the second team pitch to the east and the well-used practice playing area to the north. There are also mini-pitches here, as well as at Granby High School behind the ground and further away at Harrogate Grammar School.

However, the openness of the land can cause problems, such as those related to me by David Fotherby who looks after the three hundred and fifty junior players. Recent predicaments included local youths performing 'doughnuts' in their cars on the frozen pitches; a mass brawl between residents of the nearby Granby and Knaresborough Road Council Estates on the mini-pitches at three o'clock on a recent Sunday morning (which took fourteen police to restore order) and the same people, having destroyed the boundary fencing, using the grounds to dump their unwanted rubbish.

Fotherby also said: "As well as having to hire skips on a regular basis to cart away all of their rubbish I also have to systematically check each pitch before any play takes place for either broken glass or where people walk their dogs." No wonder the club are actively seeking to move to a new thirty-six acre site on the north-west outskirts of the town.

The old clubhouse is still standing, although unused except for storage, and next to it on the southern boundary is the main stand which, the night before my visit, had received unwanted visitors who had kicked in a number of the back panels. I counted 494 seating spaces along the wooden benches. Further on are the changing rooms situated in a single storey building.

The whole pitch is surrounded by railings with either concrete or tarmacked walkways as standing areas for spectators. At the northern end, in front of the clubhouse, is a raised concrete terraced viewing platform.

The panorama at a low level show three sides as being tree-lined, behind which are pleasant dwellings typical of those found round and about. From the top of the stand the high view looks over the suburb known as Granby and although it might have its social problems the estate is well laid out with post-war terraced homes built in local brick. From this vaunted position it is clear that considerable effort goes in to keeping the whole place as neat as possible, as befits the County Ground.

The clubhouse has four main rooms, three of which are used for sponsors and/or dining areas. One used to be a squash court, which immediately tells you the age of the building. How many rugby clubs built such courts during the fashionable age of squash, only to now use them for other purposes?

There are three bars, one for sponsors, another for members and the largest of all for the general public. The members' room has some memorabilia on the walls, but the best is in the main bar. A fourth room is purely a dining space with tables and chairs scattered around. There is an upstairs room but the bar did not seem to be in use.

It is the fourth room where general refreshments are available, presupposing you had not enjoyed one of the splendid lunches on offer each match day. Food available at the kitchen hatchway includes local pork pies as a speciality, along with a selection of rolls, pasties, bacon butties, sweets and hot drinks.

A Club Shop has been built besides the public bar and not only is it managed with great efficiency by Victoria and Pam, but they even have their own e-mail address. So wherever you are in the world you can place an order with ease.

The selection, however, is vast. There were items in club colours which I had never seen before, although I am somewhat wiser now. I think it was the 'boa scarf' which caused my initial bewilderment, followed by a 'storm top.' Oh dear, I

How Claro Road rates...

Access:	5
Car Parking:	6
Staff Attitude:	9
Comfort & Cleanliness:	8
Programme:	6
Catering:	8
Scenery & Surroundings:	7
Bars:	7
Club Shop:	10
Viewing & Shelter:	8
Total:	74 %
Ranking:	=19th

ADDRESS: The County Ground, Claro Road, Harrogate, North Yorkshire, HG1 4AG

DIRECTIONS: Claro Road is on the north side of the A59 (York-Skipton road), just off the Stray.
The nearest Railway Station is Harrogate.

PARKING: 400 spaces available at the ground.

TELEPHONE: 01423-566966

CLUB FAX: 01423-509073

CLUB SHOP: 01423-885052

SHOP FAX: 01423-545594

SHOP EMAIL: pamvictoriahrs@aol.com

WEBSITE: www.harrogaterufc.co.uk

am sounding old-fashioned. Anyway, whatever you want, they've got it - and it's all embossed.

The match programme is of thirty-two pages of which twenty-three are advertising. Of the remaining nine, three pages were editorial, two statistical and two listed the day's teams. There was no information about the players of either side.

A visit to Claro Road is always a pleasant experience and the warmth of the welcome is genuine. Should a new home eventuate it is highly likely that this hospitable club will go from strength to strength.

Riverside Park, Jedburgh, Roxburghshire, TD8 6UE.

THE best road from England to the north is the one which takes you through Jedburgh. The climb starts soon after you leave the conurbation of Newcastle and you follow the rough outline of Dere Street, the old Roman Road, towards the Scottish border.

Past Otterburn Camp and the site of the battle of 1388; onward across the junction which notes the site of Bremenivm, the Roman encampment, and upwards to the top of the Cheviot Hills. From here it is downhill for the next eleven miles into Jedburgh, one of the most picturesque towns in the Borders region.

The Romans loved it here: they set up camps all over the district. Jedburgh Abbey is a notable landmark and Mary, Queen of Scots

had a house in the town. Jed Water, which rises in the Wauchope Forest, flows by the side of the main road, past the rugby ground and joins the River Teviot a mile further up.

Riverside Park is situated north of the town between both road and river, and is a landmark for anyone travelling in the area. Speeding past, a motorist could not fail to miss the large board on top of the main stand which clearly and boldly tells the world that this is Jed-Forest Rugby Football Club.

Founded in 1884, the club are currently in Scottish Premiership Two, although the past few seasons have been a bit of a yo-yo between leagues. Continually finding top players in the region with so many other competitive sides has been quite a task for the committee.

Vehicle access to the ground is by way of a driveway in the south-west corner with spectators also gaining entry from gates at the rear of the West Stand. There is a large parking area behind the northern goal which has at least four hundred places. For those wanting a quick getaway, off-road spaces on the common land by the side of the A68 usually sees at least one hundred cars tucked in between the trees.

The scenery and surroundings are superb. From the northern end of the ground, looking through the goalposts, the twinkling lights of the town flicker in the late afternoon gloom. The view from the other parts are of woodland with the sound of rushing water breaking through any other noises. This is country sport in a quite spectacular environment.

On a match day there are always people around to help and assist. No aggressive stewards here, just plain old politeness and civility. All of my questions were answered, although no one seemed to actually know the maximum number of people the ground could hold. "It's a problem we've never had to face," said one official.

There is a main stand along part of the eastern side which seats four hundred and fifty spectators, while on the opposite terrace is a covered area which holds two hundred and fifty with ease. The southern end is a raised grass embankment which seems to be a popular spot for the club's more vocal followers. Behind the northern goal is just a flat footpath.

My biggest disappointment in walking around the arboreal boundary was to find that the club shop (sic) was situated in a rusty portakabin. Amazingly it was not open on the day of a match and all I could do was to look through the mesh protecting the window to see what was inside. Although it was obvious that clothing items were available it was a shame that I, and other visitors, could not browse through the stock. Maybe next time.

Next to the shop was a path which led up to a wooden walkway which spanned the river. An official local government notice gave a warning: 'By Order,' it read, without telling us by order of whom, 'Maximum of Six Persons to cross this Bridge at once.' In all honesty I could not think for the life of me why anyone would do such a thing as the path seemed to lead to nowhere.

There were other rusting hulks around the back of the stand one of which had 'Committee' marked on the door and others which seemed to be of use only to the groundsman.

Underneath the main stand was the clubhouse and changing rooms. There was only one bar area and it was pleasantly full during my time there. It was a large room and like so many clubs the memorabilia on the walls was stunning. There were plaques all over the actual bar with photographs and mementoes adorning every available piece of wall space.

A snack bar opened up on one wall with the usual sandwiches, pies, sweets and drinks on offer. What had been the pre-match function room, sited next door to the bar, was transformed afterwards to a dining area for both players and

How Riverside Park rates...

Access:	7
Car Parking:	7
Staff Attitude:	8
Comfort & Cleanliness:	7
Programme:	6
Catering:	6
Scenery & Surroundings:	10
Bars:	7
Club Shop:	2
Viewing & Shelter:	7
Total:	67 %
Ranking:	=34th

ADDRESS: Riverside Park, Jedburgh, Roxburghshire, TD8 6UE

DIRECTIONS: Follow the A68 South approx 1/2 mile South of Bonjedward Garage you enter a wood and the entrance to the car park is on the left. Going North, the ground is on the A68 just out of town and is clearly signposted.

PARKING: 400 spaces available at the ground.

TELEPHONE: 01835-862855

WEBSITE: www.jedforestrfc.com

spectators. There was a choice of hot meals, although the spaghetti of my bolognaise was very watery and could have been cooked a little longer.

In some ways it is cruel to be critical of the tremendous amount of voluntary work put in to clubs like Jed-Forest but it would be remiss of me if I did not suggest that there could be a fair bit of improvement to the match programme. Printing in blue type on glossy white paper is acceptable, but thirty-three pages of average advertising out of forty-four surely is not. The potential is there for a better effort.

A visit to Riverside Park should be on the agenda for anyone who enjoys the game at this level and in these surroundings. It's not a perfect venue but, at the same time, it's very acceptable.

Mint Bridge, Shap Road, Kendal, Cumbria, LA9 6DL.

THE scenery in the far north west of England is as breathtaking as any to be found in the country. Getting to Kendal is easy by using either the M6 motorway or a mainline train to Oxenholme and then changing on to the Windermere branch line. The Kendal station stop is just a few hundred yards from the Mint Bridge ground.

Whichever way you use (and I travelled by the road which crosses the top of the Forest of Bowland) the countryside opens up into vistas of rolling hills, geometrically rectangular pasture land and crazy sheep who play with the moving traffic at a whim.

The town of Kendal sits astride the River Kent, which rises in the Cumbrian Mountains and flows swiftly through the town to its mouth in Morecambe Bay. Some water is diverted to the nearby Lancaster Canal.

This is the southern tip of the

Lake District, a land of sensitive contrasts. On the Saturday of my visit, the local newspaper, 'The Westmorland Gazette', had a major front page story, with colour illustrations, of their successful 'Save Our Toilets Campaign.' The supplement section had a lead feature on the visit and performances of the Opera Company of Bangladesh. I had no idea that Bangladesh was an opera-loving country: you learn something new every day.

One of the perennial moans of local councillors is that outsiders are buying up a large percentage of Lakeland property for use as holiday homes. If the newspaper is anything to go by you can understand why. The employment section had, as its leading requirement, a quarter page advert for a cleaning job in Windermere at £190 per week 'with benefits,' whatever that might mean. Opposite, the property section did not have a single average three-bedroom house in the area for sale at under £165,000. A catch-22 situation if ever there was one.

Parts of suburban Kendal are highly attractive, although the area where the rugby ground is situated now has the Lake District Business Park (in reality, an industrial estate) towering over the pitches. Built in the early 1970s the high concrete slab buildings, with the name Heinz splattered all over them, are a blight which spoil the whole atmosphere of the area.

Reading the pages of the excellent professionally-designed programme, it is fairly obvious that club members and spectators travel to Mint Bridge rather than live nearby. Next to the ground are samples of those mortar-cladded semi-detached homes so loved in this region by local authorities. Programme advertisements offer 'luxurious homes, easy loans' and topped off by 'Kendal penthouses available at £475,000.'! I'll take two mate.

After twice going around the town's one-way system, I discarded the misleading directions given in the Rugby Club Directory and found the ground by just heading north. Shap Road was the old west coast route to Scotland before the motorway was built and in those days most travellers would have been aware of the sporting arena. It was here that John Berry, one of the Victorian era's most famous players, made his debut in 1882 for the old Kendal Hornets side.

Access is by a single entrance from a lay-by and is well marked. Opposite is Queen Katherine's School, named after King Henry VIII's surviving wife, who owned the nearby castle. The school's extensive playing fields show how flat the land is around here.

Inside the gate is a gravel surface which extends behind the clubhouse and down along the back of the adjacent second team pitch. It is an untidy parking facility which would be so much better tarmacked. Then spaces could be properly marked out and the chaotic scenes witnessed following the final whistle would not exist. At present about one hundred and twenty cars can be accommodated: properly organised this number could probably double.

Three sides around the pitch are for standing spectators. A rail exists along these sides, as well as flagstones and occasional grass banking. The eastern side possesses the stand. It is a 1930s cow-shed structure made up of wooden sleepers with corrugated iron for its backing. There are gaps between all sleepers and during the game many items were dropped between them. Luckily there were plenty of young boys around who could slip between the wood after the match to retrieve lost personal belongings.

I counted enough room to accommodate 468 under cover but in all honesty most Council safety officers elsewhere would condemn the stand as dangerous. I found five places where attempts had been made to burn it down: maybe the next might succeed.

For the match I sat with the broadcaster from Radio Cumbria.

During the lulls in play, and when he was not on air, he pointed out to me and named the various rolling hills which encircle the town. It was captivating, even more so when you realise the history of the district.

The scenery and immediate surroundings are like chalk and cheese. The view south is magnificent: look north and it's factories. The only distracting items were the numerous advertising hoardings which stated that we were watching 'The Jewson National League' (sic).

In the south-east corner near to the entrance is a very well-designed wooden hut. It is called 'The Black & Amber Shop' and inside it was as clean, neat and tidy as could be wished. A lot of items such as umbrellas, fleeces, shirts, ties, hats and scarves were available. What I did like was the special list of clothing clearly marked 'Children's Sizes.'

The only outside catering was a burger van but this was run by the club to provide limited hot food and drinks for spectators. Inside a choice of four different three-course lunches were available in the dining room, all at reasonable cost. There were two bar areas. One was fairly small and mainly for the use of members and invited guests. The other was a huge public bar with an added dining area. It would easily hold three hundred patrons.

A revolution has just taken place

KENDAL   66%

How Mint Bridge rates...

Access:	6
Car Parking:	5
Staff Attitude:	8
Comfort & Cleanliness:	6
Programme:	8
Catering:	6
Scenery & Surroundings:	6
Bars:	7
Club Shop:	8
Viewing & Shelter:	6
Total:	66 %
Ranking:	=36th

ADDRESS: Mint Bridge, Shap Road, Kendal, Cumbria, LA9 6DL

DIRECTIONS: From M6 (Junction 36) take A590 and A 591 to Kendal town centre. Then follow signs for A6 Penrith. Keep left at the 'Duke of Cumberland' and the ground is 400 metres on the left, entrance from a lay-by.
Nearest Railway Station is Kendal.

PARKING: Space for 120 cars at the ground.

TELEPHONE: 01539-734039

WEBSITE: www.kendal-rugby.com

in that the club has moved from being run by a committee to becoming more professional. It has been an amicable arrangement. We wish them well.

THE Headingley Rugby Football Club was founded in 1878; then re-formed in 1885; re-formed again in 1891, and finally amalgamated with the Roundhay Football Club in 1991 to become today's Leeds Tykes.

Originally the amalgamated club played on the old Headingley club ground, most of which is now occupied by a 'retail outlet' although some of the old pitches still exist. The short relocation north up Kirkstall Lane to what had solely been the rugby league ground in St Michael's Lane is a move which had to happen. Without a break with tradition the club would not have survived in the current professional era.

The ground itself is a base shared with a cricket ground leased to the cash-strapped Yorkshire County Cricket Club. There have been major developments in this part of the complex but they are not relevant to this article.

The old Headingley church of St Michael's towers over the neighbourhood and is a welcome sight for a traveller lost in the maze of Victorian dwellings which dominate the area. By the southern gate of the small churchyard at the top of the Lane is a fish and chip shop known to many sporting spectators. What is on offer is guaranteed to cause your cholesterol level to rise and the fatty risk of a heart attack to increase but, boy oh boy, it's worth it.

In a house opposite Gate E, in the southern part of the Lane, lived Alfred Austin who is remembered as the only journalist to have been elected as Poet Laureate. Maybe that is why for many years the press car park has been behind the wall by Austin's house.

This area is also where visiting rugby supporters are set down from their coaches and should they want a pre-match drink they are invited into The Rugby Club Bar. The large lounge is a pleasant enough place to enjoy a relaxing pint or two both before and after the game. Just inside the turnstiles here, at the back of the Southern Stand, is another bar but it is standing room only. All around the ground there is easy access to drinking areas which include Ronnie's Bar and the Sports Bar which are behind the main Northern Stand.

If a spectator wanted to eat before the game then other than the chip shop at the north of St Michael's Lane there is the 'Ugly Mugs Cafe' opposite the ticket office where 'All Day Breakfasts' are a house speciality. With this sort of competition the club have to provide a variety of options for their patrons. They offer rolls, hot pies and sweets in the Sports Bar while outside there are stalls which sell donuts (doughnuts in proper English), sweets, burgers, coffee and chicken rolls. However, the food in the area for privileged spectators looked splendid but like the Chinese in Peking at the height of the 1920s famine we could only press our noses to the windows and watch as the bourgeoisie emptied their plates.

Access to the ground is by way of an entrance in Kirkstall Lane or by various gates and turnstiles in St Michael's Lane. They are easy to find and all have special ways in for any disabled spectator. Car parking is as good as the club can provide in a suburban environment with an old pitch having been recently tarmaced in order to try and eliminate the mud created on wet days. On-street parking is possible in the surrounding residential areas, although on a big match day it could mean a lengthy walk to the ground.

The attitude of the staff and

stewards varied widely at different parts of the ground. One young lass grumpily informed me in no uncertain terms that I could not use a certain door as "there is no security guard on duty to check your ticket." As I had a pass dangling around my neck at the time I suggested that she checked it. "Not my job," came the not unexpected reply. That girl would be employed by Lord's cricket ground in an instant.

Elsewhere the stewards ranged from efficient through to those who were obviously extras from the latest James Bond movie with their black suits, cropped hair and radio earpieces. Alas, none had bulges prominent from their breast pockets.

The Club Shop is a brand new building situated next to the offices by the end of the East Terrace. Inside is a splendid variety of clothing with the logos of the rugby union, rugby league and cricket clubs on them. Sales were brisk and as much as I wanted to I could not find my size on any of the numerous items. There were also various knick-knacks and a few books, one pile of which were copies of the late Ken Dalby's splendid history of the ground published two decades ago.

The matchday magazine is now being published by a professional programme company and is a huge improvement on last season's effort.

It has 32 pages of which nine are advertisements. There are the usual articles about players and the opposition added to which are various photographs of the Leeds players, one of whom has found two bikini clad girls and is presumably taking them home.

From a comfort and cleanliness point of view I was pleased to see so many toilet facilities for women and the disabled all around the place. This is good and reflects the fact that the club want to provide as much comfort as possible for all fans and not just for men. For an established ground, cleanliness might be difficult but it is obvious that the club make a good effort to make the complex as appealing as possible.

Because of its position within the Headingley suburban area, the scenery and surroundings are nowhere near as attractive as with other club grounds. Yet there is a certain aura which can envelope a person when entering the place, especially when going up the stairs in the stand facing the cricket arena to enter the rugby stand at the top. The views from anywhere around the pitch are what one would expect from any comparable stadium.

The main Northern Stand seats 5,300 spectators in relative comfort. All enjoy good views of the action on the field of play although rumour has it that this splendid edifice is the next to be demolished

LEEDS   68%

How Headingley rates...

Access:	8
Car Parking:	7
Staff Attitude:	5
Comfort & Cleanliness:	7
Programme:	6
Catering:	6
Scenery & Surroundings:	5
Bars:	9
Club Shop:	8
Viewing & Shelter:	7
Total:	68 %
Ranking:	=32nd

ADDRESS: Headingley Stadium, St Michaels Lane, Headingley, Leeds, LS6 3BR

DIRECTIONS: From the M62 take the M621, exiting at Jnction 2 signposted Headingley Stadium. Follow the A643 (A58) Wetherby Road and, at the next roundabout, take the City Centre/Wetherby A58 exit. Almost immediately, bear left to Ilkley (A65) and the airport. At the lights, with TGI Friday on your left, turn left onto Kirkstall Road (A65). Proceed ahead for 0.75 miles (Yorkshire Television is on the right). There is a sign at the traffic lights saying "Headingley, 1.5 miles." Stay in the right hand lane. Turn right and go up the hill to another set of traffic lights at the crossroads. Carry straight on up Cardigan Road and after the pedestrian lights and bus stop, turn left into St Michaels Lane, signposted Headingley Stadium.
The nearest Railway Stations are Burley Park and Headingley.

PARKING: On-street parking around the ground.

TELEPHONE: 0113-278-6181

FAX: 0113-275-4284

TICKET DETAILS: 0113-278-6181 ext 229

WEBSITE: www.leedsrugby.com

in the cause of progress. If it is I shall miss it for I have spent many a happy hour sitting watching events unfold down below. There are two open terraces behind the goals while the covered South Stand can hold around eight thousand standing patrons.

Headingley has had a lengthy sporting history. It has an atmosphere all of its own and although many may grumble at some of its foibles, it is still a place I look forward to visiting.

Welford Road, Aylestone Road, Leicester, LE2 7TR.

A YEAR or so ago I was standing in Aylestone Road by the main entrance to Leicester Rugby Football Club. As one does I got chatting to the police superintendent who was in charge of the evening's crowd control.

One of his quotes from that night has stayed with me, for it describes the difference between supporters of the city's two codes of football. He said: "For 'A Grade' matches at Filbert Street (Leicester City's former ground) we usually have two hundred and forty police on duty with another one hundred and twenty on standby. For top games here at the rugby club other than myself there will be three constables and two wardens to direct the home going traffic."

In a way that view describes Leicestershire: town is soccer; county are rugby. Wherever you go in the countryside, people will talk to you about the 'Tigers' with many reflecting on the days before the club joined the professional era.

Leicestershire is a hunting county. In the far north-east is the Belvoir Hunt; to the north the Quorn, and south-west is Harboro Country. Recently I was at a function, held at Kibworth

Harcourt, with a number of Masters of Foxhounds. Complaints about the current state of kennels, whippers-in, coverts and lays ceased abruptly when the subject of Leicester rugby joined the conversation.

The game and the club were the second loves of their lives. I heard all about matches of yore; prep school mudbaths; inter-house contests at Uppingham and how so many of them told me to read Henry Grierson's 1924 book, 'The Ramblings of a Rabbit.' "There's a lot about early Leicester rugger in it," one MFH said knowingly. Indeed there is: not only did Grierson play for both Leicester and the Barbarians but he was also deeply involved in the early years of television.

What was fascinating was how many of them were current season-ticket holders at Welford Road. "Never miss a match, old boy," said a Wolds Farmer. "It's always a wonderful day out."

The attendance figures prove his point. The stadium has a capacity of 16,845 which is reached on a regular basis. Of that number three-quarters hold season-tickets, a figure which begs the question as to whether there are any plans for future extensions.

The ground is situated in the middle of a large one-way traffic system to the immediate south of the city. Nearby are the imposing walls of Leicester prison and the now half demolished remains of the Filbert Street site.

The shock for me on my visit was to find that the imposing Victorian structure known as the Granby Halls has been demolished and that the Leicester basketball team have had to relocate to a new venue in Loughborough. The resulting large piece of land, adjacent to the Next Stand, has been taken over by National Car Parks who charge a £4 parking fee for the duration of a match.

There is a small club parking area but otherwise it is street parking around the terraced streets near to the old football ground. Some nearby small industries charge for using their spaces, all of which are cheaper than the NCP.

Access is quite superb. Wherever you are sitting in the ground there is a turnstile or gate nearby. I counted thirty such entrances but there could be a couple I missed.

The complex consists of four covered ends. The long Crumbie Stand seats 4432 with the terrace in front allowing another 4400 to stand in relative comfort. The eastern side houses the relatively new Alliance & Leicester Stand. It still seems only the other day I saw the match against Transvaal which took place after the official opening (actually it was November 1995! Oh dear, doesn't time fly when you're having fun). This can take around three thousand spectators.

The northern structure is called the Next Stand and has 4169 seats while the West Stand sits astride a narrow piece of land between the end of the pitch and Aylestone Road. There is a temporary construction in front of the clubhouse which seats six hundred with only a few not under shelter.

With my 'Access All Areas' pass I was able to nose into every nook and cranny of the ground. What I saw has left a lasting impression for not only were the spectators catered for in every possible way but the efficiency of the club must be given due praise.

The catering is superb. At the northern end of the Crumbie Stand is the 'Pie Factory' from which a selection of hot pastry items could be obtained. Under the Alliance & Leicester Stand was the 'Curry House' which sold a selection of Indian food, and further along was the 'Wok Shop' which offered Thai specialities. There were also burger and hot doughnut vans scattered around.

However, within the clubhouse there were two large public bars at which spectators could buy a selection of various lunches. Not only did the food look extremely appetising but the range of hot meals was extraordinary. Then the crunch: the price was exactly the same as that for parking your car outside. This is a splendid policy, one which should be noted by certain other clubs who charge two to three times more for the same type of meal.

Bars were everywhere. In fact there are too many to mention. Some were for general use, others for specialist groups. I did like 'The Droglites Bar' which is for past players and their guests. They sell their own selection of embossed clothing, hats ties and plaques which do not impinge on what is sold at the Club Shop.

The main bar for seeing the club's quality memorabilia is the 'Tiger Bar' situated on the first floor of the clubhouse. 'Deano's Bar' has just Dean Richards memorabilia on display as does 'Dusty's Bar', 'Underwoods', 'Lions Bar', and 'European Bar', just to name a few. Occasionally I was a wee bit overwhelmed at what the club had on offer.

Everywhere I went there were either club stewards in neat blazers wishing to give me as much help as possible or, in the outside areas, orange jacketed stewards to guide me around.

The Club Shop was what would be expected to be provided by the country's premier club. Other than the regular clothing and ephemeral offerings I took quite a fancy to the toy stuffed tigers. Every age group is catered for here and the

How Welford Road rates...

Access:	10
Car Parking:	8
Staff Attitude:	8
Comfort & Cleanliness:	8
Programme:	10
Catering:	10
Scenery & Surroundings:	7
Bars:	9
Club Shop:	10
Viewing & Shelter:	8
Total:	88 %
Ranking:	=2nd

ADDRESS: Welford Road, Aylestone Road, Leicester, LE2 7TR

DIRECTIONS: Leave M1 (Junction 21) signposted A5460 Leicester. Immediately after exit follow signs for A563 Outer Ring Road South and East. Carry straight on at three sets of traffic lights near island, and at traffic lights for the entrance to Fosse Park. At the next set of lights turn left onto A426 Lutterworth Road towards City Centre. This becomes the Aylestone Road at next set of traffic lights, and the ground is 2 miles on right hand side. The nearest Railway Station is Leicester.

PARKING: The stadium has 100 car parking spaces with other car parks available nearby.

TELEPHONE: 0870-128-3430

FAX: 0116-285-4766

TICKET DETAILS: 0870-128-3430

CLUBSHOP: 0116-254-0077

WEBSITE: www.tigers.co.uk

manageress had no hesitation in giving me assistance at what was her busiest time of a match day.

The match programme should be used as an example of how to keep readers interested. It was only on my third perusal did I realise that what I thought was editorial content was actually advertising. Very subtle. Of sixty-four pages only four were non rugby adverts. The text was readable, slightly gossipy and provided a fair amount of useful information.

If there is to be a slight negative it is that about eighty percent of the view around the ground is of surrounding buildings or the roofs of the stands. Not a tree in sight except from the Crumbie Stand where a teasing view, looking slightly right, is of the green parkland and Victorian terraced housing the other side of Welford Road and along Waterloo Way.

The club is professional in all senses. Maybe a comparison would place Leicester Tigers as rugby union's equivalent of football's Manchester United. The club provide what the spectators need and do it in an efficient manner. They are not perfect but they come very near to it.

Incidentally, on my way home I just could not resist trying out an offering from the Curry House. It was sumptuous.

Stradey Park, Llanelli, Carmarthenshire, SA15 4BT.

THE mobile phone rang out its ghastly tune. At the other end was my bank manager. The news was good: credit references had failed to show any connection between me, money laundering or Al-Qa`eda, therefore I could now be a signatory on my wife's account. As her balance had never gone into four figures I had wondered whether all the fuss, form filling and numerous telephone calls had really been necessary.

"Where are you?" he asked.

"I'm on the road between Swansea and Llanelli," I replied.

There was silence at the other end. Then he spoke those little pearls of wisdom which indicate why he is such a valued member of our Kentish community. "So, you're in Wales then?"

He hadn't a clue that I was at the top of the Gower Peninsula and about to cross the water isthmus of the Loughor and enter Carmarthenshire. But then again, why should he?

Entered from the east, Llanelli is a series of roundabouts, retail parks and modern housing estates. The old town is a bit of a mishmash with some very appealing Victorian residences and an incredible selection of Chinese fast-food shops.

Stradey Park is an area in excess of one hundred and twenty acres with the stadium sited to the west of the open space. There are vehicle entrances from the south and east, and on none of my visits has the car park ever been full. In fact a quick assessment left me with the impression that around three thousand cars could be parked with ease.

The surprise for me in preparing this report was the obvious fact that Llanelli Rugby Club is the centre of the community. At times I found myself overwhelmed in finding out what goes on before, during and after a match at Stradey Park. To detail everything would triple my usual space so I will mention just two outside concerns.

The first is 'The Scarlets Cafe' which occupies a place in the eastern outer end of the main South Stand. Whoever got the idea of having a greasy-spoon food outlet selling 'all-day breakfasts' at two pounds each deserves praise. On match days the doors open hours before kick-off and the queues normally disperse quite some time after the final whistle. The cafe also opens during the week. I was told, unofficially, that the monthly takings are around £6000.

As a complete contrast, a large building just outside the Park's boundary is a clubhouse and bar, used on match days as an enormous pre-booked dining area. The manager allowed me to look around and the quality of what I saw was both mouth watering and impressive.

Within the ground itself there is a large social club and a lounge for sponsors and guests. These bar areas held over a thousand patrons most of whom had seats in the 4500 capacity stand. Opposite, the old 'Tanner Bank' is now the 3500 seater Calsonic Stand although the old name remains for one of the three bar areas incorporated into the building. Covered and open terracing makes up the ground capacity to 11,800.

When I went into the Control Box to talk to the Safety Officer I was immediately treated like an old friend. Chocolate biscuits were pushed my way as I was given more information than I would ever need. The lady working the closed-circuit television monitors panned in on

various parts of the ground while giving me a historical resume of its development over the years.

I wondered whether having nine bars in and around the ground caused any problems. The response was unexpected. "It's mainly lost children," I was told, "and they can always be found playing on the bouncy castles by the south-west gate."

Everywhere I went people kept asking me if I had seen the Museum. Alas, I did not have time but I saw enough of the Club's memorabilia on walls too numerous to mention. The sense of history and culture around the place was to be admired

and one framed newspaper back page with a 1956 article by J.B.G. Thomas cost me twenty minutes while I read every square inch of some wonderful prose.

The large Club Shop occupied the middle third of the outside of the main stand. The stock was massive and far too numerous to mention in detail. Clothing, books, bears, videos, mugs, pens: it was all there. A sign above the main clothes area said it all. 'If the size you want is not available then we will order it for you.' Attitude like that not only wins over fans, it makes them want to return.

Once I had settled in the

LLANELLI 78%

How Stradey Park rates...

Access:	8
Car Parking:	8
Staff Attitude:	9
Comfort & Cleanliness:	8
Programme:	5
Catering:	10
Scenery & Surroundings:	5
Bars:	8
Club Shop:	9
Viewing & Shelter:	8
Total:	78 %
Ranking:	=11th

ADDRESS: Stradey Park, Llanelli, Carmarthenshire, SA15 4BT

DIRECTIONS: Leave the M4 (Junction 48) and follow the A4138. Go straight on at the traffic lights (after about 4 miles), and after 1/4 of a mile there is a large round-about (McDonalds is in front of you) take the fourth exit for Carmarthen and Burry Bort (it is signposted Stradey Park) continue to follow the road for another 3 or 4 miles all the time following the signs for Stradey Park.
The nearest Railway Station is Llanelli.

PARKING: Plenty of car parking available at Stradey Park.

TELEPHONE: 01554-783900

FAX: 01554-783901

TICKET DETAILS: 0871-8718088

CLUBSHOP: 01554-783932

WEBSITE: www.scarlets.co.uk

pressbox I turned to the programme. It was forty-eight pages, half of which were adverts, with much duplication owing to the politically correct necessity of printing in two languages. It was a shameful waste of space as one or two of the articles were very good indeed and more of them would have been a credit.

Looking around, the scenery and surroundings were not those to generate a feeling of ease. The residential areas surrounding Stradey Park had all seen better days and their occupants gave one the feeling that a majority were housing benefit recipients.

Having said that, the overall impression was of a club which has gone out of its way to provide their spectators with every comfort. Llanelli was a very acceptable club.

LONDON IRISH

Madejski Stadium, Junction 11 M4, Reading, Berkshire, RG2 OFL.

THE new era of professional rugby means that, in order to cater properly for the spectator, new grounds have to come into use. This is what has happened to London Irish, who now play their first team fixtures at the splendid Madejski Stadium south of Reading.

In years past it was always an experience to go to the spiritual home of the Irish at Sunbury-on-Thames. The train journey from London was forever a gamble as scheduled services could arrive and depart at a whim and at any odd time. It was worse when race meetings were taking place at Kempton Park Racecourse on the other side of the Staines Road.

The Sunbury ground had an atmosphere like no other and a camaraderie unlikely to be found at the home of any of the exile clubs. Its chaos added to its charm and the blarney to be heard on match day was something else. Now that is all in the past and the club have moved along the Thames Valley to fill the spot vacated by the professional demise of Richmond.

Prior to the move to Reading they had spent one season at The Stoop, home of Harlequins, but the Irish club's professionalism and marketing successes had so shown up the Quins inadequacies that they were quickly shown the door.

The land upon which the Madejski Stadium now stands was, a decade ago, mainly scrubland sitting astride the M4 motorway and beside the Courage Brewery. The growth of Reading has been phenomenal with numerous Business Parks sprouting up along the side of the newly-diverted A33 trunk road. It is said that the wealth of a town can be gauged by the number of cranes seen on the skyline. If this is the case then Reading must be a millionaire's paradise.

And it was a millionaire, John Madejski, who had the vision to build the new complex which bears his name. The old Reading Football Club ground at Elm Park was tatty and decaying; the club needed reviving and Madejski was the man.

Once settled into the stadium the football club suddenly found it had suitors on its hands. First came a ground-sharing arrangement with Richmond Rugby Club, which ceased when the oldest club in the land (a description with which Blackheath RFC will disagree) were forcibly closed by methods which still leave a bad taste in the mouth. London Irish, who were suddenly looking for a new home in which to accommodate their ever-rising fan base, jumped at the chance to move west.

The journey by car is easy for spectators as the ground is just by a motorway junction and there are acres of parking spaces. The official car park costs £5, but a little local knowledge can find numerous spaces in local Business Parks free of charge. A shuttle bus runs every few minutes from Reading Railway Station at a cost of £1, and return buses are available for three hours after the final whistle.

The buses deposit their passengers by the entrance to the Royal Berkshire Conference Centre, which is part of the stadium. To its left is the Madejski Millennium Hotel and to its right is the Club Superstore.

No 'club shop' here; this is as good a branding outlet as any to be found. Shared with the football club, a punter can buy virtually anything they want in the London Irish brand. How about a bedspread or duvet made like a full glass of Guinness? Or maybe a fluffy dog named after Jumbo, the club's mascot, who twice gets his picture in the programme quaffing a pint of the Emerald Isle's favourite brew.

The matchday programme, at

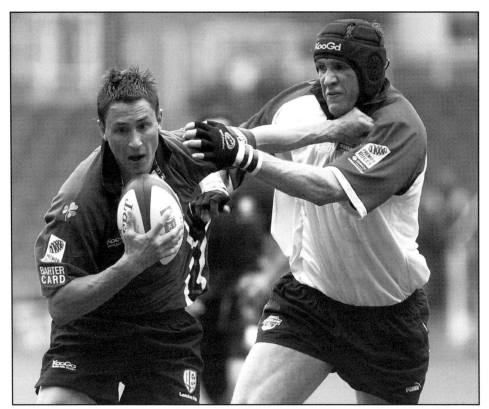

£2.50, is a fascinating production. It is unlike any other Premiership publication in that even some of the advertisements are worth reading. In seventy-two pages, editor Paddy Lennon has a wealth of information and gives the strong impression of caring about his product far more than some of the other slapped together efforts which are currently available.

The ground itself has a capacity of 24,200 and every spectator has a seat with most under cover. There are no 'ends' to the stadium as it is oval shaped. The disabled have excellent viewing facilities with each space including a seat for a helper/carer.

There is no view from the ground as it is enclosed. Scenery and surroundings are bland as befits the area although it is probably one of the safest places to watch a sporting event as there is hardly any threat of vandalism or mugging in the vicinity.

Catering is bog-standard football refreshment for the ordinary fan. However, the catering facilities for the well-heeled are very good with the quality of the lunches on offer being top rate - but expensive. Bar areas were like catering; the punters

LONDON IRISH   73%

How Madejski Stadium rates...

Access:	8
Car Parking:	9
Staff Attitude:	6
Comfort & Cleanliness:	8
Programme:	9
Catering:	5
Scenery & Surroundings:	4
Bars:	6
Club Shop:	9
Viewing & Shelter:	9
Total:	73 %
Ranking:	=21st

ADDRESS: Madejski Stadium, Junction 11 M4, Reading, Berkshire, RG2 0FL

DIRECTIONS: Leave the M4 (Junction 11) and head for Reading on the A33. At the first roundabout, take the second left onto the Reading Relief Road, passing the Stadium on your left. At the next round-about (past McDonalds) take the first left onto Northern Way and follow signs to car parks.
The nearest Railway Station is Reading - a shuttle bus service operates on matchdays.

PARKING: 2,000 spaces available at the ground and there are other car parks nearby.

TELEPHONE: 0118-987-9730

FAX: 0118-975-1091

TICKET DETAILS: 0118-968-1000

CLUBSHOP: 0118-968-1239

WEBSITE: www.london-irish.com

enjoyed their Guinness, while the diners had their wine.

Within the stadium the stewards were noticeably more relaxed than they are for football matches. For press people, such as me, the blazered men and women could not have been more kind or polite. The dichotomy was fascinating.

It is nearly impossible to recreate a rugby ground atmosphere in a football stadium, but London Irish are the nearest to achieving this out of all of the Premiership clubs. It is always a pleasure to be with the club even in its new sanitised venue.

Adams Park, Hillbottom Road, Sands, High Wycombe, HP12 4HJ.

IT was a cold and frosty Friday evening many years ago when I reported on my first Wasps match. In those long lost amateur days the club played their home fixtures at Repton Avenue in Sudbury, a stone's throw from the playing fields of Harrow School.

I had parked myself in the old wooden pressbox and at half-time timidly asked the then press officer if there was such a thing as a cup of tea available.

"Tea, dear boy, tea!" His voice cackled down the line of frozen scribes. "You don't get tea on a night like this at Wasps."

For a moment I knew how Oliver Twist had felt. Then, along the bench top skidded a number of glasses followed by two bottles of the best malt whisky.

"That'll keep you warm for the second half," barked the official's voice. "He wanted tea," he said again out loud to no one in particular.

When Wasps moved to Loftus Road in the mid-1990s to ground share with Queens Park Rangers Football Club, I did wonder if those days of whisky would still exist. They didn't: now it was brandy and black coffee served to awaiting scribblers at the half-time break. Spoil us and we'll love you forever.

My mind churned over past Wasps matches as I drove along the motorway from London towards the club's third home ground in a decade. High Wycombe, hidden in the Chiltern Hills, had only come to popular sporting notice a few years ago when the football team gained promotion to the senior leagues. Gone was the old ground in the town centre with its famous slope and memories of cup exploits. Now a new ground, called Adams Park, had risen at the end of a valley, the entrance of which was through an industrial estate serviced by the delicately-named Hillbottom Road.

The agreement Wasps have with Wycombe Wanderers Football Club is for a two-year tenure, a time factor which will be watched closely by the local authority. Planning permission for rugby to be played at the ground passed through the Council at its second attempt on "a technicality," although legal advice from the Borough solicitor suggested quite strongly that the application should have been refused, as it was at the first time of asking.

My options upon arrival were to pay car parking fees to those guarding the entrances to marked car spaces which surrounded various light industrial units, or to try my luck in the 'official' car park. If I did not want to part with a number of my hard earned shekels then I could turn the car around and go back towards the town and park in a side street a mile or more away. Maybe the walk would have done me some good, but not in the weather conditions of the day: I paid up.

My colleague, on the train from London, was not so lucky. The club had assured their supporters that buses, free of charge, would run from the railway station to the ground at twenty minute intervals for two hours before and after the game. What they did not say was that the inward journey would find passengers dumped in the middle of nowhere and told to walk the rest of the way in the appalling wind and rain. On the return journey spectators were again deposited far from the station. The Wasps publicity machine really should tell intending fans exactly what has been arranged.

Adams Park has a capacity of 10,000 according to official documents which were shown to me in the control room. On the wall in the club's boardroom the figure is given as 12,750. The main stand, again according to the safety officer, has 4990 seats for spectators. The figure given to the Football League is 7350.

Whatever the true figure, the ground provides adequate viewing and shelter for all spectators. Entry is through any of the twenty-four turnstiles. The main `Seymour Taylor Stand' seats 1267 but looks directly into the setting sun, so take your sunglasses if you ever get a ticket for this part of the stadium. Underneath are bar and dining areas for season ticket holders and invited guests. The food looked succulent and catering for quite a few hundred people appeared to cause no problem.

The north, `Greene King Stand' is for a maximum 1690 standing spectators while opposite the `Roger Vere Stand' seated 2053 in comfort. Disabled areas were provided in two places at ground level while upper stand facilities could take around forty wheelchairs if needed. The toilet facilities for the disabled were first class and immaculately clean.

Outside the ground, in the large official car park, a grand marquee provided draft beer and shelter against the elements. Next to it was an `Indian Cuisine' food stall providing various oriental delights to many satisfied patrons. Inside, each corner of the ground has a refreshment bar, along with ample toilets. The food provided was of the usual type expected in such a ground but, thank goodness, there were no burger bars with their accompanying stench.

The Club Shop was situated in a large portable hut near to the entrance of the car park. It was, naturally, shared with the football club and goods from both teams were on sale. The items were those to be expected, although the variety appeared to be more varied than usual. The disinterested attitude of the sales staff spoiled a clean record for all others on duty, from stewards through to office personnel, had been most helpful.

Once in my seat I was able to read the sixty-four page programme, of which twenty pages were adverts and twenty-one were colour pictures. My concentration was rudely shattered by the ground announcer's ten minutes of yelling into his microphone, allegedly giving the team news for those who could hear the distorted babble.

So I sat back and looked all around me. The tree-covered Chilterns provided a perfect backdrop to the relatively new stadium. It could have been restful

LONDON WASPS 70%

How Adams Park rates...

Access:	6
Car Parking:	6
Staff Attitude:	7
Comfort & Cleanliness:	8
Programme:	6
Catering:	8
Scenery & Surroundings:	8
Bars:	7
Club Shop:	6
Viewing & Shelter:	8
Total:	70 %
Ranking:	=27th

ADDRESS: Adams Park, Hillbottom Road, Sands, High Wycombe, Buckinghamshire, HP12 4HJ

DIRECTIONS: From London: Join M25 and at Junction 16 take the M40. Leave the M40 (Junction 4) and turn right over the motorway and then take first exit for A4010 (John Hall Way). Follow this road crossing three mini roundabouts until the road becomes New Road. Keep on New Road until next mini roundabout take left turn onto Lane End Road. Cross next mini roundabout onto Hillbottom Road, this will take you on to Adams Park.
From West: Leave M40 (Junction 4) and follow above directions.

Nearest Railway Station is at High Wycombe.

PARKING: Parking available at the ground or nearby.

TELEPHONE: 020-8993-8298

FAX: 020-8993-2621

TICKET DETAILS: 01494-769471

CLUBSHOP: 01494-472100

WEBSITE: www.wasps.co.uk

had we not had to endure the modern trend of having our ears bashed by unwanted noise.

But I am sure you want to know how the club of whisky and brandy now looks after its press contingent. You guessed it: four jugs of tap water and ice on a cold and windy day. C'est la vie.

LONDON WELSH

Old Deer Park, Kew Road, Richmond, Surrey, TW9 2AZ.

THE District Line Underground train disgorges its occupants at the terminus which forms part of Richmond railway station, for here is the destination for supporters of three rugby clubs: Richmond, London Scottish and London Welsh. The first two play on the Athletic Ground while the latter is at Old Deer Park.

To walk from the station along the Kew Road towards the London Welsh ground is to pass through an area of wealth, expensive restaurants and public houses of various themes. On the day of my visit the crowd in O'Kelly's Bar were cheering vociferously at the television screens which were showing a hurling match between Cork and Kerry. An Irish bar in Richmond! Whatever next!

The snobbishness of the area (where no decent property sells for under half a million pounds) is completely dissipated on arrival at the ground. "This is the place where I come to relax," said Neil Kinnock when Leader of the Opposition. How right he was, for the warmth and comfort of London Welsh Rugby Football Club is legendary on the rugby circuit.

Outside the main entrance is a large hoarding which tells any passing motorist all they would wish to know about the forthcoming rugby, cricket or hockey matches which are played on the expansive grounds. Visitors to the area are many for the northern part of Old Deer Park becomes the Royal Botanic Gardens at Kew. A Japanese Pagoda towers over the southern end of the Gardens and is a wonderful beacon for lost supporters to follow.

The eastern side of the rugby ground is the Royal Mid-Surrey Golf Course which stretches down to the River Thames, and on the opposite banks the two Battles of Brentford took place in 1016 and 1642. The Richmond Cricket and Hockey Club pitches lie to the south, while over Kew Road are Victorian terraced properties, the likes of which are usually only advertised in Country Life magazine.

Both entrances to the ground are from Kew Road with car parking limited, by necessity, to either members of the club or visiting officials. On-street parking can be found quite easily so long as it is away from the controlled restrictions which apply around Richmond town centre and environs.

The match programme is deliciously old-fashioned in that it is typeset. Written and edited with some considerable skill by club historian Paul Beken, the information is usually so detailed and interesting that half an hour can easily pass while absorbing all of the contents. Last season, Paul recalls, he had a situation late on a Thursday night when he found 111 typographical errors in his proof copy. By the Friday morning print deadline all errors had been corrected. Now that is attention to detail.

In all honesty stewarding is not really required at Old Deer Park for most people seem to know where to go and what to do. Those in situ have, over the years, become like old friends more than anything else. Cars parked in incorrect spaces appear to the most problematical part of their day and the thought of bossing spectators around would never enter their heads.

The main clubhouse bar is large, welcoming and always full on match days. In fine weather people spill on to the front lawns and usually their drinks are comple-

mented by food from the splendid barbeque set up by the offices. Other bars are for committee, guests and sponsors.

Catering is quite outstanding. Even if you are not privileged to join any of the diners in the private upstairs lounges, the facilities in the large ground floor dining area are top rate. The food on offer is of a quality and selection guaranteed to make your choice as difficult as possible. The range is from hot roast meals through to snacks or something on toast. However, if you want a recommendation, then do try the sausages as a main dish. They are distinctive Lincolnshire with herbs. Magnificent.

The club shop is situated at the southern end of the clubhouse and offers the usual items of clothing, hats, scarves and badges. Always available is Paul Beken's annual, The Roar of the Dragon, which tells the story of the previous season's exploits. Now in its seventeenth year, the annual runs on with the story of the club which was chronicled in the 1985 publication 'Dragons in Exile'.

The ground has a grandstand running along most of the western side which has a seating capacity for 1,000 spectators. Uncovered standing accommodation occupies the other three sides with 3500 fans able to watch in comfort. A tea-bar, of sorts, is to the left of the stand saving a long walk back to the clubhouse for a hot drink at half time.

To sit in the pressbox at the top of the stand needs a lot of concen-

LONDON WELSH 79%

How Old Deer Park rates...

Access:	8
Car Parking:	6
Staff Attitude:	9
Comfort & Cleanliness:	8
Programme:	9
Catering:	9
Scenery & Surroundings:	10
Bars:	8
Club Shop:	7
Viewing & Shelter:	5
Total:	79 %
Ranking:	=9th

ADDRESS: Old Deer Park, Kew Road, Richmond, Surrey, TW9 2AZ

DIRECTIONS: From M25 (Junction 12) take the M3 towards London. At the end of the M3 (Junction 1) follow the A316 towards Richmond over Twickenham Bridge. Turn left at the lights. The entrance is via double iron gates half a mile on the left. The nearest Underground/Railway Station is Richmond which is a ten minute walk from the ground. Turn right out of the station and cross over the road, follow the pavement to the pedestrian lights. Cross the dual carriageway and turn right. Continue on the pavement and the entrance is quarter of a mile down the road on the left.

PARKING: Limited Car parking in the ground but on-street parking available nearby.

TELEPHONE: 020-8940-2368

FAX: 020-8940-1106

WEBSITE: www.london-welsh.co.uk

tration while play is in progress. Your eyes can easily be averted left and upwards to see the planes stacking up before their final flight-path into Heathrow airport. Then there is the distraction of life along the Kew Road along with the arboreal atmosphere created by the various hues of the leaves on the trees which surround the whole complex. Autumn in Old Deer Park is both compelling and seductive.

Regentsholme, Regent Street, Lydney, Gloucestershire, GL15 5RN.

THE road from Chepstow to Gloucester takes you through parts of East Gloucestershire which time seems to have passed by. The journey by train is equally fascinating as you go along the estuary of the River Severn and observe the huge tidal flow.

From the south, the old Roman Road crosses the River Wye at Chepstow, passing the ancient castle and then moving over Offa's Dyke

in a trice. Northwards into the local government area of Dean Forest and Wye Valley until the site of a Roman fort indicates you have arrived on the outskirts of Lydney.

Around you is the Forest of Dean, one of the strangest parts of England. Digging for peat seems to be the most important industry after tourism, although the quality of titles found in the antiquarian bookshops of the district are probably the best in the country.

Possibly the most important sportsman to emerge from the forest was the cricketer William Murdoch. He was born in St Briavels, emigrating to Australia at the earliest opportunity, and going on to captain his adopted country for many years. Then there was Viscount Bledisloe who was the rugby club president half a century ago but who is better known in the colonies for presenting the cup which carries his name. Each year Australia and New Zealand contest his trophy.

The town of Lydney straggles up the hill, which overlooks the River Lyd. A steam railway follows the river from its source in the forest and as both descend towards the River Severn so, likewise, do the property values. The dwellings around Regentsholm are a wee bit tatty: not really worth purchasing for investment, yet by no means unacceptable.

The main problem in visiting a club like Lydney soon becomes obvious. Five times I was stopped when walking around prior to the match, each time the conversation going something like:

"Hallo. Are you a visitor?"

"Yes. I'm just taking a look at what is here."

"Good heavens. Don't do that. Come into the bar and let me buy you a beer."

I became a bit embarrassed in refusing these genuine kindnesses for no one knew who I was or what I was doing. Yet to them I was a visiting rugby fan and that was all that mattered.

Access to the ground is from the road entrance by the side of The Swan public house in the High Street or through the alleyway from Regent Street. There are three hard standing car parks at the rear of the clubhouse with overflows, if needed, at the nearby squash, cricket and football clubs. I counted three hundred spaces, but there could be more.

The pitch goes north-south and behind the goals are just standing areas for spectators. The southern view is nothing special but from the north the panoramic vista is over playing fields and the golf course which lead down to the large sandbanks at the mouth of the river.

The covered stand on the eastern side seats two hundred and underneath is kept the club's tractor and ancillary equipment. I thought the banking behind this stand was part of an old railway until I was later informed that it was a section of the town's flood defences. The only negative aspect about the outer areas is that there were no toilet facilities.

In the south-west corner is a two-storey erection which had emblazoned on it: 'Hospitality Units

Supplied By Lydney Containers.' In fact it was eight such boxes, four on each level and I must admit to have never seen such a concept before. On the day of my visit four were in use, with patrons enjoying the match from a first floor balcony. Had Gloucestershire still played county cricket here then the boxes would have a double use, for the cricket pitch is right behind.

The main stand seats 342 spectators in comfort and, as it is fairly high, the view of the playing surface is excellent. Underneath are the changing rooms and offices. Both behind and to the rear are three bar areas and a large kitchen.

The main bar has a large engraved stone by the door which tells you that 'this clubhouse was opened by Mrs Watts on 21 September 1971'. Her late husband had been the rugby club's benefactor and his generosity is still to be enjoyed.

The room easily accommodates three hundred and is serviced by a large bar. What I did find strange was that hot drinks had to be purchased from here and not from the catering service hatchway which was by the door of the second committee] bar.

It was only by chance, when waiting for coffee, that I noticed a sign on the bar wall which indicated what goods were for sale from the club shop'. Items available included jumpers, trousers, sweat-shirts, ties, rosettes, bow-ties and baseball caps. This really was very poor promotion and begs the question as to why none of the twenty-two listed club officials is designated as a commercial manager.

Alas, I found the hot food somewhat ordinary and bland. As a guest I was invited to partake in the committee's buffet and that was splendid. The third bar was heaving, it being for sponsors and their guests. It was as full as the room could be but left me with the impression that here were over five hundred people in a clubhouse, in three very distinct areas, with very little inter-mixing. Interesting.

In a corner of this latter bar was a glass case full of cups but also containing nine volumes of the club records from 1888 to date. To a sports historian these must be invaluable. In the other bars, most wall space was taken up with club memorabilia and of particular interest were the club caps, going back to 1922, which were on display.

The match programme was of forty pages, twenty-seven of which were adverts. It was a standard issue and provided as much infor-mation as any onlooker would need.

All around me during and after the match I found people who were chatty, friendly and in some instances, very interesting. Once

LYDNEY 71%

How Regentsholme rates...

Access:	8
Car Parking:	9
Staff Attitude:	10
Comfort & Cleanliness:	8
Programme:	6
Catering:	4
Scenery & Surroundings:	7
Bars:	8
Club Shop:	3
Viewing & Shelter:	8
Total:	71 %
Ranking:	=24th

ADDRESS: Regentsholme, Regent Street, Lydney, Gloucestershire, GL15 5RN

DIRECTIONS: From M4 (Junction 11) follow the A40 to bypass Gloucester and follow the A48 south (signposted Chepstow) for approx. 16 miles. Take the exit signposted Lydney off the A48 bypass and drive down the hill into Lydney. Immediately after passing the second Pelican crossing turn left into Swan Road. Continue approx. 200 yards past the garage and turn left into the car park immediately in front of the Cricket Club.
From M48 and Chepstow follow the A48 (north) for approx. 8 miles. Approx. 1 mile after passing through Aylburton you'll come to a roundabout. Take the first exit (signposted Lydney), follow the main road and at the foot of the hill turn right into Swan Road. Continue approx. 200 yards past the garage and turn left into the car park immediately in front of the Cricket Club.

PARKING: Car park adjacent to the ground.

TELEPHONE: 01594-842479

FAX: 01594-843064

WEBSITE: www.lydneyrfc.co.uk

Emma, the local journalist, had told a few of the committee that I was from 'Rugby Times' I soon heard which sections of the paper they liked more than others. You need not guess which feature they liked the best.

MANCHESTER

Grove Park, Grove Lane, Cheadle Hulme, Cheshire, SK8 7NB.

AS the Wilmslow Road takes you south, further and further from the bustle of the city of Manchester, so the east Cheshire countryside opens up invitingly. The car speeds past what used to be the hamlets of Gatley, Heald Green and Cheadle Hulme before coming to rest in Grove Lane. Here is Grove Park, the not quite new home of Manchester Rugby Club.

The move from their original ground in Moor Lane, Salford some thirty years ago was forced upon them by the local authority who had grand plans for the site. We all know what Councils are like: say one thing, do another.

So the community development failed to materialise and to save the site becoming a wasteland it was taken over by Salford Amateur Rugby League Club. What irony in those days when the two codes failed to acknowledge each other's existence.

Now there is a long driveway leading to the large clubhouse which is shared with Cheadle Hulme Cricket Club and Grove Park

Squash Club. The late-1960s structure is in dire need of a makeover: the paintwork, peeling from the wooden slats, and the unkempt service area spoil what is basically a well-designed building.

By the entrance to the cricket ground changing rooms is a small sundial memorial, complete with a poppy wreath, which records the loss of players in both wars. Alas, the plasterwork was crumbling away. Surely a little attention to detail would not go amiss here.

It was I who was the attention just at this moment, for suspicions had arisen in the clubhouse as to my ulterior motives in jotting down notes in my meanderings around the place. Twice I was followed and where I had been all locks and bolts were duly double checked. Forgive me: my `Raffles' days are now behind me.

The inner car park had 47 spaces marked out; the gravel areas along the driveway held 150 cars and for big matches the second pitch can hold a further 200 vehicles. There is also a separate designated section for disabled cars by the side of the squash courts as well as an ambulance bay.

Just around the corner from this bay was the Club Shop, situated in a portakabin, with the door facing the four turnstiles. On offer were the usual tracksuits, tops, shirts, and

various rugby wear. What was noticeable was that the sizes varied from small to 3XXX: they must be big boys around these parts.

Inside the clubhouse there was a choice of three bars and an eating area. The walls were all covered with team photographs and in the committee room various items of an historical nature were behind glass. One item, a 1912 dinner menu, caused a lengthy discussion between visiting committeemen who were unsure of its correct detail. Sorry chaps, too late to change it now.

Outside there were a number of `Emergency Exit' signs on appropriate gates which were sited around the ground. The duty Safety Officer told me that all access/exit entrances were checked twice: before and during a match. It was excellent to hear such planning.

Once inside the gates I stood and took in the splendid view. My presence was already known for the man selling programmes came up to me and said: "Don't forget to let your readers know that we are the best gatemen and programme sellers in the League."

The ground has a capacity for 4,750 spectators. The Harry Ryle Memorial Stand, opened in 1975 and still in pristine condition, seats 250 in comfort. Opposite, on the eastern side, is `The Pacemakers Stand,' a raised covered terrace for 750 fans. There is plenty of spare land behind this and other terracing should the club ever wish to expand and as my pressbox colleague remarked: "I have no idea why Sale Rugby Club have never looked here in their search for a new ground."

To the left of the Stand is `The Grove Park Grill' serviced by a group of the most pleasant ladies you could ever wish to meet. Not only that, but for once I found a ground where greasy junk offerings were banned and only quality food and drink were sold. No smelly burgers; no burnt sausages; no onion stench to hang on to your clothes. Eat your heart out Fanny Craddock for even you would have been surprised by this.

Forgive me if I exude my delight for where else would I be offered a variation which started with freshly cooked hot beef or pork in a large bread roll (with stuffing and apple sauce optional) and finished with Irish coffee. Naturally, the ground coffee was percolated with a choice of blends. Next door was a covered bar which sold draft beer from various kegs as well as the bottled variety.

When I eventually reached the pressbox I was able to read the match programme. It comprised thirty-six pages of which only six (and that is being generous) had any reading material.

Then I could sit back and enjoy

MANCHESTER 75%

How Grove Park rates...

Access:	7
Car Parking:	7
Staff Attitude:	8
Comfort & Cleanliness:	8
Programme:	3
Catering:	10
Scenery & Surroundings:	10
Bars:	8
Club Shop:	6
Viewing & Shelter:	8
Total:	75 %
Ranking:	18th

ADDRESS: Grove Park, Grove Lane, Cheadle Hulme, Cheshire, SK8 7NB

DIRECTIONS: From the M62/M61, Join M60 and follow signs to Stockport. Exit M60 (Junction 3) and follow the A34 towards Wilmslow and Congleton. Follow the A34 for approx. 2 miles and at the second roundabout take first exit towards Bramhall. Follow Stanley Road for quarter of a mile - Grove Park is on the right 50 yards after The Smithy pub.

PARKING: 400 spaces available.

TELEPHONE: 0161-485-3733

FAX: 0161-485-1115

WEBSITE: www.manchester-rugby.co.uk

the view. The sky was a mixture of clear blue and black clouds. Rainbows came and went as did aircraft descending into nearby Ringway Airport. Looking south over Chester's Croft all that could be seen were trees, some so azure in colour that they nearly blended in with the darkened sky.

It was restful; it was fresh; it was invigorating. It was Manchester Rugby Club.

The Greenyards, High Street, Melrose, Roxburghshire, TD6 9SA.

SOME years ago I wrote a book about my search to find the most perfect place in Britain in which I could live. After spending two years wandering around this island of ours I had whittled a short list down to three localities. By a very narrow margin Melrose came second and that was only due to its sparse public transport facilities.

The Scottish Borders is a most civilised part of the world and at its heart is Melrose. Situated some forty miles south-west of Edinburgh, the town sits astride the River Tweed and is on the Southern Uplands. The splendid road system which serves the area means easy accessability to virtually anywhere.

When researching my book I stayed in the town for a few days and found the natives to be friendly, cultured, educated and kind. All around the immediate vicinity are to be found National Trust of Scotland houses and gardens, and, of course,

Melrose Abbey itself is one of the most historic buildings in the country.

The centre of Melrose is surrounded by large Victorian houses with the old railway station hotel a focal point. At the lower end of the main street is The Greenyards, home of the rugby club. Founded in 1877, a little later than most other of the famous Borders teams, the club has provided many of the players for Scotland's international sides since then.

One of the first things which strike you on seeing the outside of the ground is the lack of a fence or wall to keep non-paying customers at bay. Watching, as I did before a game, not one person tried to avoid honouring their dues to the gatemen and the only free access was gained by a collie dog.

The front entrance is beautifully designed in local stone and the gates and turnstile boxes have the club's initials emblazoned on the top. Just inside the ground, on the left, the club crest has been carved into the sandstone banking.

There are a number of car park spaces in the front yard and some at St Mary's School at the rear of the stand, but these are for players and officials. Directly opposite the main gate is a large community parking area where the signs welcome you to use the facilities free of charge.

The only request is for patrons not to drop any litter or to make a mess. This really is unnecessary as the town has no litter: it also has no graffiti, no aggressive youths and no undesirable elements.

For the disabled, a gate at the western end of the Greenyards gives access and allows them to drive up on to a mound from which they can see the whole playing surface and to watch the match in the comfort of their own vehicles.

Three sides of the ground are open grass banked mounds and although twelve thousand spectators have crammed in for past important matches only half of that number would be allowed in today. The main stand, on the eastern perimeter, has 1174 seats under cover and above these, along the whole length of the roof, is an enclosed mansard expanse which is for the media. This pressbox is one of the finest in which I have ever had the privilege to work.

The view from this exalted position is superb. Straight ahead is a sloping green and on the top is St Cuthbert's Parish Church. All around the rising vista is of multi-roomed detached Victorian dwellings: these desirable residences, when they come on to the market, are priced at figures an inner-Londoner would pay for a garage.

On the right side of the expansive driveway is a large

portakabin which has been converted into the club shop. It is not that often I walk through the door and give an involuntary gasp at what is on the shelves. It was not the quantity which amazed me but the quality. Here was a selection of top brand sportswear at very affordable prices. My purchase of a 'Pringle' brand embossed sweater gave me change from a ten pound note.

It was not only the sport and leisure wear in club colours which caught my eye. A local artist, John Martin, had sketched a series of views of the ground and these coloured drawings were for sale both as framed or unframed prints. There was also the usual selection of mugs, key-rings, ties and pins - but no fluffy bears!

The clubhouse behind the stand contained a mass of memorabilia. Wherever you looked there were walls, shelves and cabinets full of the history of the club and its people. The entrance vestibule celebrated Ned Haig who had been the brains behind the founding of the 'Melrose Sevens' back in 1883.

However, by far the most interesting items were in a glass fronted case on the wall by the side of the middle bar. They were replicas of two published sets of the laws. The first stated 'Football' as agreed 'by a levee of the sixth [of Melrose School] on 28 August 1845'. The other was of 'The Laws of Football' as written by Rugby School in October 1856. A comment argues that the Melrose rules were copied by Rugby.

There are two large bar areas within the clubhouse. One is solely

How The Greenyards rates...

Access:	9
Car Parking:	9
Staff Attitude:	10
Comfort & Cleanliness:	8
Programme:	8
Catering:	8
Scenery & Surroundings:	10
Bars:	8
Club Shop:	10
Viewing & Shelter:	8
Total:	88 %
Ranking:	=2nd

ADDRESS: The Greenyards, High Street, Melrose, Roxburghshire, TD6 9SA

DIRECTIONS: Travel on A68 take A6091 junction at roundabout signposted Melrose. Travel along A6091 for approx. 1 mile then turn right at junction B6374 signposted Melrose. Travel into Melrose, the ground is not difficult to find as it is at the bottom of the main street.

PARKING: The main car park is just across the road from the front entrance, plenty of street parking is also available close to the ground.

TELEPHONE: 01896-822559

FAX: 01896-822993

WEBSITE:
www.melroserugby.bordernet.co.uk

for drinking while the second, much larger, bar has half devoted to the catering outlet and for general dining. Before the game there are the usual pies, rolls and confectionary on sale but afterwards a good selection of hot meals are readily available. Upstairs are two function rooms with kitchens. Outside, by the terracing, is a mobile hot food van.

The forty-four page programme is a regular issue expected at this level of the game. Printed on glossy paper, the subjects of the advertising caught the eye even before any editorial was perused. The boutiques, outfitters, furniture shops, business advisors, hotels and car dealers were all a cut above the norm. Add to this an incredibly detailed dozen pages of news and everything you wanted to know about the club and the town was in your hands.

The standard and quality of information and assistance given to me by the secretary and officials at the club was certainly an experience I would like to have everywhere I go. Nothing was too much trouble even though they had no idea I was preparing this article. It was more than a pleasure to go to Melrose Rugby Football Club. Indeed, it was a privilege.

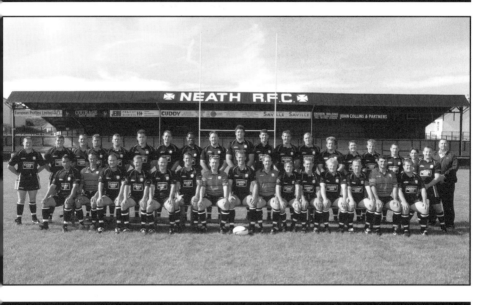

The Gnoll, Gnoll Park Road, Neath, SA11 3BU.

AS I write there are nine Premier Division rugby clubs in Wales. Rumours say that this figure could possibly fall to five as quickly as the beginning of next season. *(Subsequently, this has proved to be the case)*. With the current health of the Welsh Rugby Union in such a very poor condition who knows what might soon become of the game in the Principality.

Neath Rugby Football Club is currently one of the nine, albeit in the bottom four of the 'club grading'

as being proposed by the WRU's restructuring working party. The idea being floated that Swansea absorb Neath to create a 'Provincial Club' is being fought tooth and nail by the Neath Board *(unsuccessfully)*.

I knew little of this battle as I drove to the ground. From Swansea I went through Llansamlet and Skewen to cross the Vale of Neath before arriving in the town. The centre is dominated by a supermarket whose buildings have intruded into the now paved main

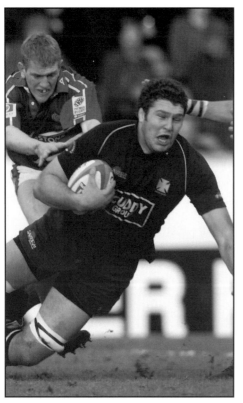

street. Contrasts abounded: In the middle of the small shopping district were two public houses diagonally opposite each other. The Angel was attracting young people by the score as its unoffensive music gave a warmth to the autumnal bite of early evening. The Castle, in contrast, was obviously the home of those of advancing years who dawdled over their drinks while time passed them by.

A few hundred yards further up the road and The Gnoll rugby ground came into view. My first impression was that here was an old football ground of four decades or so ago. The back of the main stand ran along the pavement parallel to Gnoll Park Road. It had occasional orifices into which people disappeared and then, seemingly miraculously, reappeared. One of these semi-basement hideaways contained the Club's shop. It was well stocked and had a lot to offer for all members of the family, so long as your favourite colour was black.

Once the car had been parked in one of the maze of terraced side streets, a stroll along Gnoll Park Road revealed late-Victorian property of a standard highly sought in other parts of the country. One three-storey home was for sale. As I saw later in an Estate Agent's window the place: "... has four main bedrooms, three living rooms, two toilets, a study, bathroom ..." In parts of West London the price would be in seven figures. In Neath it was £44,995!

Directly opposite this bargain was the entrance for people like me. I wandered in and started chatting to the two officials who were in charge of the gate. They directed my gaze across the playing area and upwards. "That is the Gnoll," I was told. "The old Gnoll House used to be there on top of the hill and this pitch was part of the grounds." They were both generous with their time and the history lesson which included the news that, "the old basement has recently been excavated and they've discovered the wine cellar." Heaven forbid.

The ground has a capacity for 7,500, with the main covered stand seating 1,500 in reasonable comfort. Around on the left at the northern end is open uncovered terracing, while a temporary covered stand occupies the western side. Behind this is the ground of Neath Cricket Club and the building which is Neath Leisure Centre. Car parking is available here but only for players, officials and sponsors.

The remaining covered terrace has part of its rear sealed off as it has, somewhat oddly, become the resting place for the remains of hundreds upon hundreds of old plastic bucket seats. Had this been a football stadium officialdom would have had the terrace sealed off and closed to the paying public.

Two burger bars serviced the needs of hungry adults while the younger patrons had a field day at the sweet kiosk which offered a fascinating array of things, all of which in time would rot their teeth.

The bar set up was strange. Once inside the ground it appeared impossible to get a drink as all doors to the clubhouse were locked. Entrance was from the main road only, so goodness knows who made that rule.

As I wandered around the ground prior to kick-off I got the feeling that the stewards were too busy gossiping at times to look after the patrons. In my final few yards I came up against two jobsworths who took great delight in giving me a lecture for not having a club pass with me.

"Jonathan [the press officer] gives them out. Go and get one from him," were my instructions. Alas Jonathan knew nothing of the said accreditation so I returned to the gate, waved my Barclaycard under their noses as if it was the correct pass, smiled sweetly as I was motioned through and carried on compiling my report.

Shortly afterwards, while seated in the pressbox, I started to read the matchday programme. It was deceptively informative with some trenchant comments and a superb thought provoking article on the way Welsh rugby is currently being directed. The editor deserves praise for an excellent production.

As I was reading my eyes were suddenly distracted downwards. Coming from the tunnel beneath me were the evening's sponsors and their guests. They walked in pairs towards their allocated seats, many with cigarettes dangling from their mouths, and without meaning to be cruel I said, instinctively, to my journalist neighbour from the Western Mail: "Goodness me, look at all of those sunbed suntans." He nodded knowingly for there was much mutton dressed as lamb.

NEATH · 54%

How The Gnoll rates...

Access:	6
Car Parking:	3
Staff Attitude:	4
Comfort & Cleanliness:	6
Programme:	8
Catering:	4
Scenery & Surroundings:	6
Bars:	3
Club Shop:	8
Viewing & Shelter:	6
Total:	54 %
Ranking:	48th

ADDRESS: The Gnoll, Gnoll Park Road, Neath, SA11 3BU

DIRECTIONS: Leave the M4 (Junction 43) and follow the A465 into Neath. At the roundabout, follow the signs to Cimla and Pontrhydyfen. At the traffic lights, go straight ahead until you approach a second roundabout. The Gnoll is directly ahead.
The Nearest Railway Station is Neath - approx. 15 minutes walk.

PARKING: On-street parking available nearby.

TELEPHONE: 01639-769660

FAX: 01639-769661

CLUBSHOP: 01639-769667

WEBSITE: www.neathrfc.co.uk

Then, looking upwards, I saw a much more acceptable sight. The autumnal colours of the trees on the hills produced a delightful backdrop to the game in which the Welsh All Blacks (as Neath are known) strolled to an easy win.

I expect that my views might not be appreciated in certain quarters but the frustration at finding one of the oldest rugby clubs in such a state of uneasiness was depressing. To make matters worse, of the two scoreboards only one was working and on the occasions the public address system actually operated we all got constant apologies for the inability to broadcast any music.

I left with a feeling of melancholy for here was one of the game's traditional clubs, uncertain as to its future and appearing to be rudderless as a result.

Monks Lane, Newbury, Berkshire, RG14 7RW.

IF you ever mention the name of the county of Berkshire in a sporting context the odds are that the discussion will turn immediately to horse racing. For in the far north west of the county is the village of Lambourn where racing stables abound and trainers are in abundance.

Nowadays Berkshire can also offer top flight football in Reading as well as rugby union through London Irish. Both play at the magnificent new Madejski Stadium near to the motorway corridor.

It is only the rugby people who recognise that a few miles further west along the old A4 trunk road lies Newbury, a town whose club lie in a healthy position in National Division Two.

A decade ago the club made the decision to relocate to the outskirts of town to a new purpose built site in Monks Lane on the edge of the southern suburbs. They moved in during the summer of 1996 just after winning promotion out of the regional leagues.

Further success followed on the

field of play while off it the complex grew and the organisation gained a reputation so high that the powers that be at Twickenham decided to test the water by awarding the club a Divisional match against a touring team from Queensland.

From this success the RFU have awarded regular representative fixtures culminating in the club being given all four England Under-21 matches last season

Monks Lane is the connecting link between two main southern approaches to Newbury. One side is of good detached residential property while the other used to be rolling countryside. Now that the rugby club have moved in

thousands of tons of soil have been moved to create a landscape which is pleasing to the eye and which has not detracted from its original aura.

Such huge banking has been created that a slightly 'bowl' feeling is given when you climb up any of the three grass slopes. The fact that the local authority have granted a safety certificate for 7500 standing spectators speaks reams for the good design of the ground. So far the record crowd has been 6100, and that still left plenty of room for people to move around with ease.

Access is by the main driveway down to a tarmacked parking area which holds three hundred cars and a dozen coaches. On busy match days an overflow car park exists, from another Monks Lane entrance, which takes over one thousand vehicles. A pathway then connects with an entrance gate situated on the eastern boundary. Should even more space be needed then it is available a bit further down the road.

The whole area gives an air of tranquillity and this is perhaps why the club has built up a reputation as a place for people or companies to hold conferences, functions or celebrations.

As you enter the clubhouse a large reception area opens up. To your left is the 'Fitness Studio' (gymnasium to you and me) which, according to the club's brochure, offers "quality instruction and equipment" with "free workout classes for rugby club members." Looking at the beer bellies wobbling by the bar this generous offer has been slow to be appreciated.

To the right of the main entrance is the members bar, a well adorned place with tasteful colours and decor. This is the 'Langdon Lounge' where the committee entertain their guests before matches with food being available from a portable hostess.

The Club Shop opens up on the left and is a credit to the volunteers who run it. The place was spotless with all items of clothing neatly arranged either on a wall display or hanging from various racks. There were the usual accessories such as ties, caps, hats, bags and badges readily available.

At the far end of the hallway are two further doors. To the left are the twelve changing rooms while everyone else goes right along a short corridor to the entrance to the 'Kickers Sportsbar'. This is a large room with a raised area for seating while a lengthy bar serves thirsty spectators.

At the far end is the refreshment bar which provides all manner of hot meals, pizzas, pies, sandwiches and drinks. The speciality here are the pasties, made by a local bakery and extremely succulent.

Upstairs are a number of small offices with the 'Wickens Suite' being the main dining area. There is a bar here which services the needs of up to one hundred and sixty patrons who can eat in comfort. When disco-dances are held this figure rises to two hundred and twenty. This function room has dividers and can easily convert into three rooms for business conferences.

Outside, the main stand is attached to the gym and although there are only two hundred seats under cover the club do erect portable seating for big matches. What was noted was the excellent under cover facilities provided for disabled supporters.

NEWBURY 77%

How Monks Lane rates...

Access:	8
Car Parking:	9
Staff Attitude:	9
Comfort & Cleanliness:	7
Programme:	6
Catering:	7
Scenery & Surroundings:	9
Bars:	7
Club Shop:	8
Viewing & Shelter:	7
Total:	77 %
Ranking:	=14th

ADDRESS: Monks Lane, Newbury, Berkshire, RG14 7RW

DIRECTIONS: Leave the M4 (Junction 13) and take the A34 bypass exiting on the A343 towards Newbury. After approx. 2 miles turn right into Monks Lane. The ground is on the right. The nearest Railway Station is Newbury.

PARKING: 300 spaces and overflow car park available.

TELEPHONE: 01635-40103

FAX: 01635-40533

WEBSITE: www.newburyrfc.co.uk

The match programme is a forty page affair in full colour and printed on glossy paper. Although many pages are devoted to advertisements the editorial content is very informative with player information being exactly what is required.

The club are developing the complex slowly but surely. Like all rugby committees they have plans for the future. With the amount of land available those plans might actually come to fruition.

Kingston Park, Brunton Road, Kenton Bank Foot, Newcastle, NE13 8AF.

WAS it really only twelve years go that the modern Newcastle club came into existence? The old Gosforth club is now little more than a memory as so much has happened in the meantime.

When the current ground opened in 1990 there were just 450 seats: with the current new building work completed over 5400 can be seated under cover, all having splendid views of the pitch.

Whoever made the decision in the late 1980s to site the new rugby ground at Kenton Bankfoot must have been a visionary for surely the ground is one of the best placed in the major leagues. Car access is so easy from the Great North Road with Kingston Park Station providing a Metro tram link right into the centre of Newcastle.

The area around the ground was mainly developed during the last decade. Housing, designed for modern living in secluded Courts and Closes, is accessible from public transport connections through a network of walkways and open spaces. The now obligatory retail park gives a choice of supermarkets while nearby public houses offer pre-match lunch deals which "include a free pint of locally-brewed beer".

Vehicle entrance is gained from Brunton Road from where a series of stewards direct your car into one of the 600 spaces. If the car park is full, which happens on a regular basis, then street parking poses little difficulty.

Outside the main entrance to the superbly designed and practical clubhouse/conference centre is a trailer which complements the excellent club shop housed in the main building on the eastern side of the ground. The mobile facility is in operation to make sure everyone entering the ground is aware of all the branded products on sale. The usual selection of shirts, jumpers, hat, scarves and tracksuits were all available. There was also a large basket full of miniature bears, all dressed in Falcons' colours.

On the grass outside, the club had erected two bouncy castles for children. Each was properly supervised.

The main clubhouse entrance is staffed on matchdays by immaculately dressed men and women. They were more than helpful to me with one going out of his way to make sure that I saw everything I needed to see. There were a number of corporate hospitality bar and lunch areas with the food being served smelling succulent.

What then caused me much amazement was to go into the ground and to find that this quality food was on offer to the regular punters. The fact that this was available stunned visiting fans who immediately took advantage by forming lengthy queues along the concourse under the South Stand. For once there were no smelly burgers or hot-dogs: now it was the pungent whiff of hot roast beef, lamb and pork with, of course, sage and onion stuffing plus apple or mint sauce.

To help everyone enjoy themselves the club had thoughtfully provided a Skiffle Group to play in the hour before the start. To help them along their way a smiling steward kept serving the band members pints of Guinness. It was all so civilised.

Also under the South Stand were two large bars with others available in the 3800 seat West Stand. Prior to the completion of the new facility, patrons were satisfied while building work was in progress coutesy of two beer marquees at each end of the North Stand. After the match one of the large dining areas in the clubhouse reverts to a public bar and within ten minutes of the final whistle it was packed out.

My wandering around the ground came to a prolonged halt

under the North Stand as I spent some time observing a number of junior matches taking place on the back pitches. I, along with many parents, sheltered from the rain as we watched the games in progress. It is always good for the soul to see tomorrow's generations showing off their sporting prowess. I got chatting to one of the fathers standing besides me. "Of course," I said, "when I was his age ......" I'm afraid I rather droned on. The man was most polite but you could see that in his mind he had already nominated me for the next 'Bore-of-the-Month-Award'.

I must mention the stewards. They came from a company called Protector Events Stewarding. Everywhere I went, both inside and outside the ground, they were polite, helpful and extremely friendly. Spectators remember stewards' attitudes: these were a credit to the club who had hired them.

The pressbox is halfway up the splendid new West Stand. Before the start I read through the sixty-four page programme. Although twenty-two pages were advertising there had obviously been some effort put into its production.

Then I looked up and realised what a delightful view there was to the north and east. The woods of Woolsington Park absorbed the

NEWCASTLE 78%

How Kingston Park rates...

Access:	8
Car Parking:	9
Staff Attitude:	10
Comfort & Cleanliness:	7
Programme:	6
Catering:	9
Scenery & Surroundings:	8
Bars:	7
Club Shop:	7
Viewing & Shelter:	7
Total:	78 %
Ranking:	=11th

ADDRESS: Kingston Park, Brunton Road, Kenton Bank Foot, Newcastle, NE13 8AF

DIRECTIONS: Follow the A1 to the Newcastle Airport junction. Take the Kingston Park exit off the roundabout, go straight ahead at the next two mini roundabouts. Pass under the bridge and take the right turn into Brunton Road. The ground is on the left after the bend. The nearest Railway station is Newcastle, then use the Metro to either Kingston Park or Bank Foot stations.

PARKING: 600 spaces at the ground.

TELEPHONE: 0191-214-5588

FAX: 0191-286-0824

TICKET DETAILS: 0870-085-6060

CLUBHOUSE: 0191-214-2811

CLUBSHOP: 0191-214-2833

WEBSITE: www.newcastle-falcons.co.uk

noise of planes landing at nearby Newcastle Airport while the undulating farmland to the east stretched all the way to the Havannah Nature Reserve. The soothing music over the tannoy system was like manna: it was just so relaxing.

Just before the end of the match I saw two policemen and a traffic warden turn up at the main gate. They were to organise and direct the traffic flow as the crowd departed. They were not needed as the stewards had everything under control.

Kingston Park is a superb ground in which to enjoy watching rugby. It is a credit to the professional game.

Franklin's Gardens, Weedon Road, Northampton, NN5 5BG.

THE day I went to Northampton was so cold that even the local brass monkeys stayed in by the fire. It had not been at all chilly when I left London's Euston Station on the Silverlink Flyer. As we went north through such quintessentially-English named towns such as Kings Langley, Hemel Hempstead, Leighton Buzzard and Milton Keynes so it became obvious that the outside temperature was falling.

By the time we reached the station at Northampton the opening of the carriage doors sent a blast of Arctic air into our faces. The ticket collector at the barriers was most informative. "Football's off, rugby's on," he called out to the passengers. I already knew about the football as my office had phoned me an hour earlier. That kick-off had been scheduled for noon so my intended double-header had been booted in to touch.

"You'll be able to have a wander around the town, then," said Stan from the warmth of the office, "before you go to the rugby, then."

Why do people nowadays say

'then' at the end of each sentence? It's like little girls who chant 'really, really' in mantra fashion in every utterance they make.

Suddenly I was halted in my tracks. What was this? A plaque on a wall by a gate telling me that the railway station is built on the site of the old town's castle. This gate being all that remains from the 1060 AD structure. There was more, much more as I started to enjoy my visit. There were plaques and historical buildings everywhere. The local Heritage Society have done a splendid job in making the town of considerable interest.

Then came the coup-de-grace. At the top of the pedestrianised Abington Street was a statue to a former local member of parliament. As I went to read the inscription I noticed another statue further down the road. As it was in the middle of a one-way system which divided Wellingborough Road and Kettering Road, I had to dodge between the speeding vehicles to get to it.

What I had come across was the memorial statue to Edgar Mobbs, the former Northampton and England rugby international who, at the beginning of the first war, had formed the Mobbs Own regiment which comprised many sporting personalities. It is the centrepiece of an unostentatious war memorial and garden. I sat down and enjoyed the tranquillity of the place: outside noises being completely ignored.

Then it was back down the hill, through the shopping area and into Peacock Place to visit the 'Saints Shop', one of the Club's two retail outlets. After looking around I took a copy of the constantly updated 'Merchandise Brochure' and sat outside to read what was available. Everything you could think of, appeared to be the answer. The selection was vast and presented under various titles: Clothing and Accessories, Ladieswear, Kids and Babies Stuff, Leisurewear and Stocking Fillers. My favourite was the settee cover made up to look like a Saints flag. This is rugby commercialism at its very best.

The walk to the ground took me past Norman churches and the location archaeologists say was the original settlement some seventeen hundred years ago. I slipped and slid over the River Nene bridge before arriving by the front driveways in Weedon Road. If only something could be done about the small conclave of 1960s shops, flats and gruesome bingo hall which create such a poor initial impression: for Franklin's Gardens really is a nice place to go.

The recent rebuilding of three of the stands has been a remarkable achievement by the club. The reaction by the fans has been the sale of 5946 season tickets out of 11,500 seats available. The ground

capacity of 12,600 has already been reached for two matches and the comfort and sighting levels is high wherever you go in the stands.

Access is so easy that you can enter from almost any of the entrance points. The ground is designed for convenience and is unlike many others in that you can walk around without inhibition. Car parking, on fine days, is virtually unlimited although when the ground is wet this becomes limited. Street parking is plentiful and safe.

To say that the ground is 'user friendly' would be somewhat of an understatement. There is so much to occupy adults and children alike both before and after a game that it is a bit of a struggle to leave. The Lakeside Village area behind the Southern Stand springs easily to mind.

A pond occupies land at the rear of the stand and then the place explodes into life. There are numerous food stalls with the longest queue being for the 'Hot Pasties' outlet; bars are plentiful with the 'Crooked Hooker' (for former players and invited guests) the most popular; the bouncy castles were very tempting for some non-children, while the face-painting stall served mums as well as kids. The 'Junior Saints' shop sold horrible things such as bubble-gum, chewy bars and flavoured fizzy pop with the Club Shop restricting the numbers being allowed in for safety reasons.

Should you have wished to go

NORTHAMPTON 85%

How Franklin's Gardens rates...

Access:	9
Car Parking:	8
Staff Attitude:	9
Comfort & Cleanliness:	9
Programme:	8
Catering:	9
Scenery & Surroundings:	6
Bars:	7
Club Shop:	10
Viewing & Shelter:	10
Total:	85 %
Ranking:	5th

ADDRESS: Franklin's Gardens, Weedon Road, Northampton, NN5 5BG

DIRECTIONS: From the South - leave M1 (Junction 15A) and follow signs towards Sixfields, past the Sixfields Stadium on the right to the major roundabout. Take right turn onto A4500 for the Town Centre. Follow signs to Saints car park. From the North - leave M1 (Junction 16) and follow the A45 to Northampton and follow signs to Town Centre at major traffic island. Then follow the directions as above.
The nearest Railway Station is Northampton.

PARKING: Large car park and on-street parking available.

TELEPHONE: 01604-751543

FAX: 01604-599110

TICKET DETAILS: 01604-581000

CLUBSHOP: 01604-599111

WEBSITE: www.northamptonsaints.co.uk

indoors for drinks or refreshments there were bars in both the Church's Stand and Tetley's Stand. For diners The Sturtridge Pavilion provided meals along with forty private boxes. There are also function rooms (the Rodber Suite, Heroes and the Captain's Suite) in the Tetley's Stand which can accommodate up to seven hundred as well as providing bar meals and a restaurant. It is all overwhelming, but brilliant.

There is a quarterly club magazine, 'Black, Green & Gold,' which is widely distributed and intends to inform as well to entertain. The programme, 'Saints Review' is tightly edited and cuts out on waffle and padding seen so regularly in other similar productions. It is sixty-eight pages of good reading.

From a professional point of view Franklin's Gardens is a superb place to work. The pressbox has room and facilities are easy to access. From a spectator's angle this is a modern ground for the modern era. There is hardly anything anyone could do make any improvements.

Ireland Avenue, Beeston, Nottingham, NG9 1JD.

THE Midland Mainline train service from London can go to either Derby or Nottingham when it gets to the junction at Long Eaton. Situated by the side of the River Trent and right on the triangular boundary of Derbyshire, Leicestershire and Nottinghamshire, the immediate area is known more for its speedway racing than any other sport. Developers have got hold of the track and are holding the local

Borough council to ransom in order to obtain planning permission.

The road going north-west has Beeston as its next town and here is the home of Nottingham Rugby Football Club. They too are hoping to get developers involved with their land, but that is for the future.

I alighted from the train at Beeston Station to be met by pools of blood, for a cyclist had just been attacked on the platform and his bike stolen. Along with others I comforted the poor man until the paramedics arrived only to have them argue with me (why me?) for allegedly directing them to the wrong platform.

As I walked towards Beeston town centre two things became apparent. The first was the preponderance of young men with black eyes or other fighting facial injuries: the second was the number of grossly obese women in both shops and the pedestrian precinct who were shouting at the tops of their voices at their children. The owner of 'Books & Things' in Station Road excused them by telling me: "It's poor around here."

There may be poverty around about (although the north of the county is in a far worse state) but there are also some fine parts of Beeston. As you walk from the town to the ground you go through the 'St John's Grove Conservation Area' which is one of fourteen conservation zones set up by the Borough of Broxtowe.

Back in 1809, following the enclosure of the land around Beeston, the Grove was allocated to the vicar of St John's Parish Church. In 1878, the Beeston Land Society acquired the land and from it twenty-eight large sub-divisions were created. One is now known as the Dovecote Lane Recreation Ground which houses an ornamental garden, a play area for children and a bandstand. Another (initially owned by Leslie Birkin) is on the opposite side of Queens Road and is the rugby ground.

A year earlier his brother, Alick, had returned to Nottingham from Rugby School and had formed a rugby team. From then, until 1956, the Birkin family retained close connections with the club their ancestor had founded.

Nowadays the only access to the ground is through Ireland Avenue, a street of unimpressive residences. At the end are two entrances, the right one leading to a football pitch where I spent some time watching Wollaton play in a Midland Amateur Alliance fixture. The other opening is a driveway which takes you past the old rugby clubhouse to parking areas at various spots around the perimeter. The main car park takes one hundred and thirty vehicles with room for another fifty elsewhere.

The pitch goes from east to west with the changing rooms in the north-east corner at the side of the mainly unused old clubhouse and bar. This is not the only structure left in disrepair around the place, which is sad, for the ground has seen far better days. As kind as officials were to me on my visit it could not disguise the fact that an air of tiredness existed.

Two rows of conifer trees broke

up some of the poorer views, hiding a disused malting factory behind the south-east fence and from some of the noise from the main railway line along the southern boundary. The variation of trains was amazing: six companies with eight styles of livery and going to all parts of the country. The club have two pitches at the western end with the second team using the main one.

The new clubhouse looked to be a late 1970s structure built from a design so loved by post-modernist architects of that period: trendy but impractical. The first thing which hits any visitor are the wall paintings: one sign on the outside and an internal mural, neither of which would look out of place in North Belfast. Maybe it's because the address refers to Ireland.

When the place was built it was during the boom in the game of squash and therefore three courts were erected as the back half of the structure. None of these are now in use. Two are currently used as gymnasia for the players with the other being covered by a false ceiling and converted into offices and the club shop.

The shop had a good range of clothing available, along with hats, ties, scarves, socks and all other such ephemera. Opposite was the catering hatch which offered, alas, little to excite the palate. There was a main bar which was well patronised but others which were locked up. When I queried this I was informed that match attendances were not high enough to justify their opening.

There were various honour boards and pictures on the walls but the best memorabilia was to be found in the only 'executive box'

NOTTINGHAM 61%

How Ireland Avenue rates...

Access:	5
Car Parking:	7
Staff Attitude:	8
Comfort & Cleanliness:	5
Programme:	7
Catering:	4
Scenery & Surroundings:	5
Bars:	6
Club Shop:	8
Viewing & Shelter:	6
Total:	61 %
Ranking:	=43rd

ADDRESS: Ireland Avenue, Beeston, Nottingham, NG9 1JD.

DIRECTIONS: Leave M1 (Junction 25) and follow A52 towards Nottingham, at the first roundabout turn right onto B6003 and then left onto A6005. Follow this road onto Queens Road West, turn right after the bus depot onto Dovecourt Lane and right onto Ireland Avenue.
Nearest Railway Station is Beeston.

PARKING: 180 spaces available at the ground.

TELEPHONE: 0115-925-4238

FAX: 0115-925-4255

WEBSITE: www.nottinghamrfc.co.uk

which was open on a match day. Here a group of supporters get together in the end room of a wooden hut which is sited by the south-west pitch boundary.

The main stand is on the northern side and has 468 seats under cover, all with good sight of play. However, by far the best view is enjoyed by spectators opposite, who stand on the clubhouse roof. Without shelter, and sometimes windy, these diehards can watch the match from an exalted position.

The pressbox was excellent and provided good working facilities. Prior to the match I read the twenty-eight page programme. At first I was unimpressed but on subsequent readings it has proved to be a mine of information.

A visit to Ireland Avenue is a bit like the curate's egg: good in parts. I found a group of keen enthusiasts running the show but I did have to wonder if, as the game becomes more professional which in itself creates more pressure, as to whether the club can survive in its current form.

Edge Hall Road, Orrell, Wigan, WN5 8TL.

THE area around Wigan has seen quite a number of sporting upheavals over the past few years. The most important moves were the relocation of the football club from Springfield Park and the rugby league club from Central Park. Both transferred into the splendid new stadium built at the Robin Park Sports Complex.

The owner of both clubs, Dave Whelan, is the former Blackburn Rovers fullback who turned his hand to business with spectacular results. A year or so ago he added Orrell Rugby Union Football Club to his portfolio. The occasional fixture allocated to the new stadium did not go down too well with the punters, so the club has retained its base at its old ground.

In easy to describe terms the Edge Hall Road site sits astride the junction of two motorways: the M6

which goes north-south and the M58 which is east-west. Only when there are few spectators in the place does motorway noise become a distraction. Otherwise you would hardly notice the thousands of vehicles which pass by during the 80 minutes of a match.

Situated within a mass of roads comprising century old terraced artisan dwellings, the Orrell playing fields occupy a site long coveted by construction companies. Some fields have already fallen to devel-

opers, with acres of smart new narrow brick buildings surrounding two parts of the club's boundary. The American-style names given to these estates are downright stupid for the area.

When you get to the boarded-up frontage of the old Orrell Railway Station, with its proud 'Lancashire & Yorkshire Railway Company' nameplate gathering rust on the front arch, you know the rugby club is but yards away.

Access is gained through a short

driveway, and parking for large vehicles is on the tarmac behind the remains of the burnt out clubhouse. Other parking, for cars, is on three other parts of the ground, including on the fourth of the four pitches which make up the playing fields.

The western end, behind the goal, is now a level site, the remains of last August's fire having been cleared away. The general opinion is that the conflagration was the result of a bungled burglary rather than a straight out arson attack. Whatever the cause, the splendid clubhouse is no more.

Visitors were recommended to go next door to 'The Station' public house for lunch and pre-match drinks, an arrangement willingly agreed to by the landlord. He has set aside a bar for rugby people and his splendid £3.50 lunch is highly recommended. Because of the situation and the pub atmosphere, the camaraderie of the place was endemic and I found myself with numerous new friends within a short space of time. This is an excellent temporary arrangement for which the club deserve praise.

Inside the ground, behind the southern covered terracing, are two vans: one is a portable bar, the other is for hot food and drink. Again, most acceptable in the circumstances.

The south covered standing area holds two thousand fans, with the western terrace (also stepped concrete) taking the same again. The main stand is relatively new and occupies most of the northern side. It has covered seating for a fraction under a thousand spectators. The only thing really missing on a day as cold as it was on my visit was a stall selling hot drinks, but that is more of an observation than a criticism.

Behind the stand is the first of three other pitches. Standing looking at the view I was constantly distracted by a tinkling sound. I eventually found it came from the garden nearest to the stand where the owner had placed a series of Saharan camel bells, the ones which blow in the wind to warn desert travellers of impending visitors.

Rows of trees, originally planted as wind breaks, run behind both the eastern and southern ends. They break up the flatness of the pitches and provide a pleasant view from the numerous pitched roofs on show.

Although the club do not have a shop, at present, to sell their merchandise, arrangements have been made with two major local retail outlets for club goods to be sold through them. The programme shows in detail what is currently available, and having seen the old club shop prior to the fire it is only fair that an average rating is given in this exceptional instance.

The programme is a most profes-

ORRELL   69%

How Edge Hall Road rates...

Access:	7
Car Parking:	7
Staff Attitude:	10
Comfort & Cleanliness:	7
Programme:	5
Catering:	7
Scenery & Surroundings:	6
Bars:	7
Club Shop:	5
Viewing & Shelter:	8
Total:	69 %
Ranking:	=30th

ADDRESS: Edge Hall Road, Orrell, Wigan, WN5 8TL.

DIRECTIONS: Leave M6 (Junction 26) and turn left at the end of the slip road onto the A577. Turn left at the lights at the Stag Inn on to the B5206 and after approx. 400 yards turn left again at the lights and left again after 400 yards into Edge Hall Road.
The nearest Railway Station is Orrell.

PARKING: 250 spaces at the ground.

TELEPHONE: 01942-774000

sional job, comprising thity-two pages of which half are advertising with the rest colour photographs and editorial. Proof checking was not perfect, neither was some of the spelling, which you should expect to get in a two-pound publication.

From the moment I arrived at Edge Hall Road, I met friendly faces and helpful people. The stewards could not have been kinder and within a few minutes the club's Operations Manager had taken me into the temporary press room and put a hot drink into my frozen hands.

To top off a most pleasant visit, the players turned on a marvellous match. Hopefully it will not be too long before a new clubhouse has risen from the ashes.

When it has I shall tell you all about it.

Cross Green, Otley, West Yorkshire, LS21 1HE.

ABOVE the grey houses and narrow streets of Otley rises the Chevin, a great hill ridge with a glorious panoramic view of the surrounding countryside which is known as Wharfedale.

At the top the scene is one of the river gleaming among the woods and meadows, and down in the valley below is the market town of some 12,000 inhabitants.

There is much to see in Otley. An ancient bridge of seven arches; numerous old coaching inns; a church which has its origins in Norman days and which possesses a monument in the churchyard set up in the memory of the 30 men who were killed when the Bramhope railway tunnel under the Chevin collapsed.

The rugby ground in Cross

Green is virtually in the centre of town, a short walk away from many of those inns which sell a variety of ales, most of which are brewed within the West Riding of Yorkshire.

The last Sunday of each month sees a 'Farmers Market' take place in the Market Square. The fish, vegetables and other foods on sale are so fresh and pure that members of the younger generation, raised on junk food with chemical additives, should be aware of the consequences of eating such unadulterated produce.

A short walk from the main road brings spectators to both the turnstiles and the Peter Creswick Memorial Gates, a splendid example of the work of a local wrought ironsmith. This is the only access to the club but is perfectly adequate for all needs.

A small car park bestrides the entrance walkway, with the main parking area opposite in Bremner Street where, by arrangement, over 400 vehicles can park within the confines of the Craftsman Tools factory. Disabled patrons have a special parking area within the ground.

In some respects the words 'fresh' and 'pure' could well be applied to the ambience of the ground. Once through the gates an initial view of the playing area and surrounds is breathtaking. From the open Western Terrace the panorama offers Ilkley Moor and moving around the ground is like having a circular tour of the Wharfe Valley.

Opposite the entrance are the changing rooms and turning right brings a notice saying 'Otley Study & Sports Development' at the doors to a collection of single storey rooms. Further on is the Otley Squash Club, behind which is the Otley Cricket Club.

Some of the western terracing comprises local stone, duly stepped but worn down over the years. The section some twenty yards each side of the halfway line is of raised wooden slats above which is a television gantry, also wooden. The view away from the pitch is over the cricket ground and a cemetery.

The north terrace looks over to the Chevin and behind is a small paddock with sheep and chickens. Absent-mindedly I looked at a ewe and said, "hello". It looked up at me and replied: "baa". That was the sum total of our conversation.

The East Stand runs for three-quarters the length of the pitch and seats exactly 499 spectators. At the north end is another television gantry but on the day of my visit the two BSkyB cameramen refused to use them and insisted on placing themselves at the top of the main stairs so blocking the view of many fans and all of the press.

When it was suggested that they move to the gantry their replies

need little guesswork. There is covered terracing behind the southern goal. The ground capacity is 8,500. But in reality about 5,000 could watch in comfort.

What was so soothing about the day of my visit was the sound of the Otley Brass Band playing a selection of popular songs. There was no ear splitting cacophony coming from a souped-up sound system. This was pleasant and relaxing. As one spectator said to me: "This is like going back to my youth. It's all so civilised."

The clubhouse had a kitchen area with a dozen volunteer ladies looking after all of our food whims and fancies. There was a selection of pies to be had with chips and mushy peas, along with home-made cakes, the speciality of which was a mouth-watering fruit cake. Outside,

a group of men were in charge of a barbecue which also had soft drinks and sweets on sale for the children.

There are two bar areas, the main one of which had a food stall at one end and a bar which ran nearly the length of one wall. What was so interesting was that the smaller bar had numerous team photographs on the walls while in the larger area there were proper professional trophy cabinets which displayed various historical rugby items.

Inside the clubhouse dining area, in its own room, was the Club Shop. On sale was a variety of clothing such as t-shirts, polo neck sweaters, jumpers, fleeces, shirts, cardigans and anoraks; a selection of which were actually in my size! There were also umbrellas, scarves, ties, shorts and hats. Not a bad selection for a non-Premiership club.

OTLEY   80%

How Cross Green rates...

Access:	9
Car Parking:	9
Staff Attitude:	9
Comfort & Cleanliness:	5
Programme:	9
Catering:	8
Scenery & Surroundings:	9
Bars:	7
Club Shop:	8
Viewing & Shelter:	7
Total:	80 %
Ranking:	8th

ADDRESS: Cross Green, Otley, West Yorkshire, LS21 1HE.

DIRECTIONS: Cross Green is on the left hand side of the road leading to Pool-in-Wharfedale and is quarter of a mile from the town centre.
Nearest Railway Station is Menston.

PARKING: 60 in ground, further parking for 400 available opposite.

TELEPHONE: 01943-850142

FAX: 01943-461180

WEBSITE: www.otleyrugby.co.uk

Both the clubhouse and ground were in an immaculately clean condition. However, unless you were back in the bars there were no toilets worthy of the name although one men's area (for it was just some corrugated sheets stuck together to give privacy and erected on the walkway behind the main stand) did exist outside. It was horribly unhygienic.

Everywhere I went around the whole club complex I found committee people and volunteer helpers to be courteous, kind and efficient. Little things make a day, such as a lady from the kitchen rushing after me to say that I had been charged twenty pence too much for my coffee and pressing a coin into my hand with apologies.

All around the club were copies of the first issue of this season's Newsletter. It was informative, as was the match programme, a forty page effort comprising news, club messages and ten pages of advertising. Like many National Division One programmes this production by Peter Thompson gave me much more news than any Premiership effort.

Otley is a rugby club to be enjoyed. It has a charm of its own while perfection is not very far away.

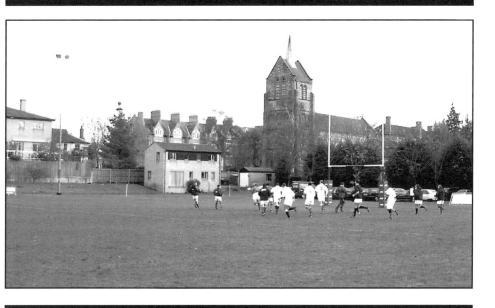

THE train journey to Oxford becomes more civilised the further away you get from London. The 'Thames Trains' turbo express gathers enough pace to go through the awful industrialised western suburbs in the quickest time possible. Then Slough, an even more depressing area, is passed before any recital of John Betjeman's poem about the place can be completed.

Soon Reading comes into view with its new silicon valley business parks and then the rustic civilisation of Berkshire and Oxfordshire takes over. The River Thames dominates the countryside as you pass through Pangbourne, Goring & Streatley, Cholsey, Culham and Radley. Then, as the train slows down, the spires of the university city start to dominate the skyline.

From the station entrance a right turn puts you into Park End Street and if, like me, you love old English food, the delicatessen shop on the other side of the road will take your one pound coin in exchange for a bag of the most delicious home-made chocolate coated tiffin.

The walk through the town centre, over Magdalen Bridge and into Iffley Road takes you past some of the more ancient colleges. Balliol, Brasenose, Oriel, All Souls and Corpus Christi are there or there-abouts with St Hilda's on the borders of Christ Church Meadow. It is this north side of the expansive flood plain of the River Cherwell upon which the University sports fields are situated.

Just before the rugby ground is the athletics stadium. It was here on that famous day in 1954 that Roger Bannister became the first British athlete to run a mile in under four minutes. It has been completely redesigned since then and now stages more football matches than any other sport.

The street entrance to the rugby club is possibly one of the most picturesque imaginable. A short tree-lined path widens to allow spectators to either go through the turnstiles or ticket booths into the ground. A sloping walkway leads to the rear of the pavilion on the left or straight ahead takes you around the back of the northern goal area. The main gate is off Jackdaw Lane and from it the driveway leads up to the vehicle entrance behind the old stand. Around 250 parking spaces are available on match days with Range Rovers and four-wheel drives occupying most of them.

A couple of years ago for their match with the Australian tourists, and with the benefit of two temporary stands, the club had an attendance of just under six thousand. In normal circumstances the ground capacity is three thousand, of which exactly half are seats under shelter.

The main, western, stand houses not only the changing rooms but the offices of the Director of Rugby, his coaching staff and administration. The 'Club Shop' is also to be found along the main corridor although you will need to ask someone in the office to unlock the door so you can see what is available. The selection is remarkably varied and includes polo shirts, fleeces, baseball caps, beanies, sweaters, ties and t-shirts. Sizes range from dwarf to giant so no one should go away disap-pointed.

On match days there is a marquee which provides lunch for sponsors and their guests. If a gate-paying punter fancied a hot drink or a sandwich then they would have to

leave the ground and walk through to Cowley Road for any refreshment. There is absolutely nothing other than a tent for beer and, allegedly, wine. This is a dreadfully poor state of affairs and even the bar in the Members' Pavilion had no food to offer.

To the right of the main stand is a television gantry and swinging around behind the southern goal is another area for vehicle parking.

The recently appointed groundsman has a house in the south-east corner behind which is Bannister Close, a 1980s development of town houses. Views from the dining areas and upper bedrooms encompassed the whole playing area and many heads can be seen bobbing up and down during play.

The Eastern Stand is utilitarian, low in height, but providing a splendid view over into Christ Church Meadow. Sitting in one of the seats on a fine autumn day is as relaxing as could ever be imagined. Even the old RAF four-propeller planes going overhead cause no real disturbance.

In the north-east corner lies a splendid pavilion circa 1920 and a memorial. This is the member's domain and it has a warmth and camaraderie known only to those who have been through their privileged system. To watch a match while seated in the wicker chairs at the front of the glass covered conservatory is akin to being transported back to the days of the empire.

Alas, the sad part is the memorial so recently erected to remember Ian Tucker. It was just six years ago, while playing for the University against Saracens, that he received the head injury which was eventually to prove fatal. The metal plinth and sculpture are most tastefully designed and appropriate for the intended memory.

Behind the northern goal is a splendid scoreboard, and behind that a row of tall trees which mark the boundary with the athletics arena. The view looking down the pitch is of Victorian Oxford. Dominated by a Catholic church on Iffley Road there are two roads of terraced houses, originally artisan but now worth a small fortune.

As usual, time in the pressbox gave me the opportunity to peruse the match programme. It was of 24 pages of which half comprised quality advertising. Even so, there was much of interest.

A match at Iffley Road is always a pleasant experience. However, it is also like being at a crazy concert: when the signature tunes of a few hundred mobile phones go off at the same time even Beethoven would have been hard pushed to have created such a cacophony.

PLYMOUTH ALBION

Beacon Park, Beacon Park Road, Peverell, Plymouth, PL3 2JP.

PLYMOUTH is a naval town so it is not unusual to see the grey shapes of British warships at anchor in some part or another of the River Tamar. From Beacon Park, the home of Plymouth Albion Rugby Football Club in the suburb of Peverell, the hills of Cornwall can also be seen in the far distance over the river. On the day of my visit a destroyer occupied the background view for part of my walk back to the city centre down the hilly thoroughfares which comprise, in the main, mid-wars suburban dwellings.

To a stranger, South Devon gives the impression of being a little confused with its identity. Ivybridge, to the east of Plymouth, is a splendid duplication of an Australian rural community in the State of Victoria; while the suburbs of the city scream confusion.

Around the Beacon Park ground are steep streets full of endless rows of monotonous terraced properties while at the back part of the north-east corner a peep through the bushes will reveal the latest example of high density detached housing meant for the upwardly mobile two income generation. Alas, the famous old rugby ground could easily find itself occupied by such bland property and renamed 'Paradise Heights.' Heaven forbid. The whole place is in its death throes and kind as one would wish to be, these reports must reflect the true state of affairs at the time of inspection.

There are three access points to the ground, two of which comprise a single turnstile (or 'Turn Styles' according to the Club's site map), while the third is through a vehicle entrance so sanded that children were making sandcastles while their parents were in a nearby marquee called 'The Village'. This space is for visiting coaches and a dozen or so cars belonging to the privileged few. On-street parking is essential and there is no difficulty in finding spaces in which to park with safety.

The majority of Beacon Park smelt of decay. The reasons for this are many, not least a proposed move to the Devonport Services ground or to a brand new stadium at Brickfields. But once the traumas of such promised moves, or alleged new super-duper local council funded promises, start to fade quickly into the distance then at least some preparation work should be done on your current venue. The excuses I heard during my visit left a strong impression of someone

having taken their eye off the ball.

The main stand with seating for five hundred had standing areas to each side. The north-west corner part had terracing of railway sleepers and on the wall at the rear were three smashed light fittings, all with exposed wiring! The northern end was bare of anything except a walkway. The covered terracing on the eastern side is called the 'Supporters [no apostrophe] Stand,' which had a plaque to commemorate its reopening in September 1987 by Mrs Wakeham. The unkempt walkway in front no doubt had its mass of weeds trampled in to the ground by the day's spectators.

Behind the southern goal was a quite impressive clubhouse and further round was a hospitality marquee, none of which had public viewing areas. Declining buildings and portakabins, most of which still had some use, wrapped up the south west corner.

There has been a considerable effort made to cater for all levels of spectators whether they be corporate sponsors or ordinary fans. There are two large marquees at each end of the western side. The northern one is called 'The Village' and hosts what the club call "a Guinness and traditional Irish stew bar". Admittedly the food was excellent but the punters were not those expected to flock in to eat and drink. In fact the word 'creche' came more to mind than the word 'tavern.' The young wives with their plates of stew gossiped endlessly, and from listening in to one lengthy conversation I now know which nursery school is their recommended choice.

The southern marquee was for "pre-booked meals" as I was told. The first floor clubhouse dining room was similarly occupied so where, I wondered, did the punters eat? The answer was that they all queued for cornish pasties from the front of a portakabin which, miraculously, opened its side flap to reveal a kitchen. My image of glorious Devon milk with my coffee soon dissipated as I realised my drink included powdered milk and so was soon disposed of behind the stand along with other rotting effects.

There are two good sized bars within the clubhouse and another at the end of the hospitality marquee. The ground floor bar has been thoughtfully decorated with mementoes of the Club's history and a lot of time and effort has gone into making the place as interesting as possible. Upstairs, in the small area not occupied by sponsors, the bar was packed. Service was prompt and it was obviously the meeting point for many of the home fans.

In one corner was the club shop. Although it was small, the variety of goods on offer was excellent. All

shapes and sizes were available in the selection of shirts, fleeces, sweatshirts and other items of clothing. Also on display were videos, woolly hats, bow-ties and much else, including club trumpets, many of which became an instant irritant when being blown during the game.

Communication is always important and the club had gone out of its way to make sure that every spectator entering the ground had a 'site map' of how to find their way around. The 32 page

PLYMOUTH ALBION 59%

How Beacon Park rates...

Access:	5
Car Parking:	5
Staff Attitude:	7
Comfort & Cleanliness:	4
Programme:	8
Catering:	6
Scenery & Surroundings:	4
Bars:	8
Club Shop:	8
Viewing & Shelter:	4
Total:	59 %
Ranking:	=46th

ADDRESS: Beacon Park, Beacon Park Road, Peverell, Plymouth, PL3 2JP.

DIRECTIONS: From the A38 from Exeter take the turning for the A386 (Outland Road) junction and follow the signs for the city centre. At the first major set of traffic lights turn right into Ham Drive, and then left into Langstone Road. Langstone Road leads into Beacon Park Road and the ground is situated on the right.
The nearest Railway Stations is Plymouth.

PARKING: On-street parking nearby.

TELEPHONE: 01752-777454

FAX: 01752-793273

WEBSITE: www.plymouthalbionrfc.co.uk

programme was good value with a number of pages of text, some of which might just reappear unaltered in each issue.

Plymouth Albion is a well supported club in solid rugby union territory. The playing side has gone from strength to strength in recent years. If only the same could be said for the facilities.

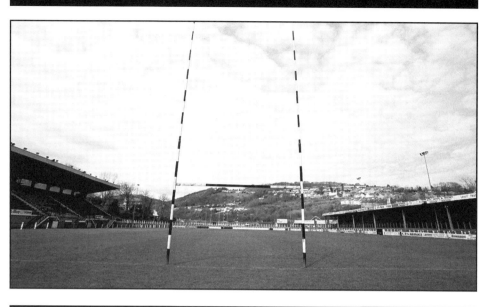

Sardis Road, Pontypridd, CF37 1HA.

UNTIL the great metamorphosis took place (circa 1984) which changed the face of British industry forever, South Wales had always been associated with coal mining. Now, as you drive along the dual carriageways which hug the side of the valleys, there is hardly a mineshaft in sight. Those you do see are monuments to the past.

Today the valleys have reinvented themselves into either light industrial estates or local versions of Silicon Valley. This change is particularly prominent as you drive north from any of the main artery junctions of the M4 motorway.

The route to Pontypridd along the valley of the River Taff can be done quickly on the main road, or slowly through places such as Taff's Well, Nantgarw, Glyntaff and Treforest. Suddenly you are in the town and going slowly past the huge high wall upon which sits Pontypridd railway station. This is an important junction which sees northern bound trains go along three separate branch lines ending up in either Aberdare, Treherbert or Merthyr Tydfil.

The rugby ground sits on the lower side of a hill by the side of the River Rhondda, a tributary of the River Taff. It is but a short climb up Sardis Road before a right turn takes you into the parking area outside the clubhouse. Only forty cars can be accommodated in this area but exactly opposite is a huge corporation car park which can take over seven hundred vehicles. At the lower end of the ground the suburb of Pwll-Gwaun comprises a maze of terraced streets all of which are suitable places to leave your car.

This northern access is where the television outside-broadcast vans seem to be at virtually every match. However, they do not intrude on the four turnstiles. At the opposite, south, end there are sets of turnstiles each side of the large clubhouse complex.

The ground itself is beautifully old-fashioned. The main, western, stand gives splendid views right across the town and of the antiquated trains as they leave for their journeys north along the high brick viaducts. The lights of Coed-Pen-Maen, Point Sion Norton and Trallwng flicker in the cool night air, for most of modern-day Ponty's matches have an evening kick-off.

The northern terrace is uncovered but nearly three thousand patrons can shelter in comfort under the East Stand roof. The ground capacity of 7861 also includes those in the temporary sponsors boxes which are strangely sited behind the southern goal but right in front of the clubhouse windows.

Catering is hit and miss. The food available in the clubhouse and from some of the outside catering vehicles is little short of grease wrapped up in a sugar-bun. The fish and chip van advertises prices which would be considered expensive in London, let alone a Welsh provincial town. But on the good side was the tea-hut run by club's lady volunteers which served splendid pies, sandwiches, cakes and hot drinks.

Bar facilities were numerous and excellent. Three-quarters of the area underneath the main stand was given over to public and members' lounges. The clubhouse had slightly less space but was more crowded. There was no waiting time at any bar for however many people wanted to purchase drinks at the same time an appropriate number of staff would quickly appear to assist.

The Club Shop had an entrance

from the clubhouse bar by way of a set of doors which to get through meant ducking your head to avoid hitting it against a low hanging lintel. Once inside you notice a well-stocked clothing section and the usual ephemeral items. There was, however, a book for sale telling the story of recent seasons. As I had not seen it before, I made enquiries and found that it was only available through the club: to me it seems a strange way to market your product.

As I wandered around the ground I found an atmosphere of anticipation for the match. I have no idea whether it was the tannoy system's continual playing of Tom Jones singing his entire repertoire of songs which caused such expectation. I would have thought it would have done the opposite but, then again, I'm not Welsh.

Stewards were helpful and the police friendly: they were only needed later on to direct home-going traffic. Families were prominent and at no time would any parent have been fearful for their child's safety. After the game youngsters (and some fathers) hustled around getting autographs from co-operative players, some of whom were still on the playing arena. Had this scene been at a Premiership football match most would have been arrested under the 'Safety at Sports Grounds Act'. Thank goodness common sense prevailed here.

Once in the pressbox I had time to look at the forty-eight page programme, a third of which was

PONTYPRIDD 70%

How Sardis Road rates...

Access:	7
Car Parking:	7
Staff Attitude:	8
Comfort & Cleanliness:	7
Programme:	6
Catering:	5
Scenery & Surroundings:	8
Bars:	9
Club Shop:	6
Viewing & Shelter:	7
Total:	70 %
Ranking:	=27th

ADDRESS: Sardis Road, Pontypridd, CF37 1HA.

DIRECTIONS: Leave the M4 (Junction 32) and follow the A470 to Pontypridd. The ground is situated in the Town Centre near the Sardis Road roundabout.
The nearest Railway Station is Pontypridd.

PARKING: 40 Spaces available at the ground with other car parking nearby.

TELEPHONE: 01443-405006

FAX: 01433-407087

WEBSITE: www.pontypriddrfc.co.uk

advertising. It contained some interesting articles and comment pieces but was nothing spectacular.

I was then distracted by some shuffling along the press seats. Former Welsh international Gerald Davies had arrived. He writes for 'The Times' and needed to find a worktop. He asked if I would mind moving up a couple of seats, which I did.

He then offered his hand and said: "You are a gentleman and a scholar."

I was puzzled. We had never met before, so how did he know?

RICHMOND / LONDON SCOTTISH

The Athletic Ground, Kew Foot Road, Richmond, Surrey, TW9 2SS.
(Shared ground of Richmond and London Scottish since 1878)

SOUTH WEST London is a rugby stronghold, no more so than around the areas of Richmond and Twickenham. Here, either side of a great meander in the River Thames, are the homes of a number of clubs as well as the headquarters of the game itself.

The area of Richmond is a cut above anything else locally, with both property and shops being in a class of their own. Around the entrance to the railway station are a number of estate agents. A glance at what they have to offer makes you realise that there are some heights in life which can only be reached by those who either used to work in the City or who have inherited wealth. When you see riverside flats going for £1.2 million, it's time to look away.

Richmond town centre is noted for its characteristic public houses;

quality women's clothing outlets; theatres of distinction and restaurants of considerable excellence. Behind the main emporiums are alleyways full of quaint antique shops, trendy boutiques and sandwich bars offering food, the likes of which usually need a continental taste to appreciate.

Then there is Richmond Green with its old pubs, nearby river frontage and remains of the old Richmond Palace. Walk north past the Community College, cross Twickenham Road and there in front of you is the big sign which says: 'Welcome to the Richmond Athletic Ground (RAG): Home of Richmond and London Scottish [Rugby] Football Clubs.'

As an alternative you could walk down Kew Foot Road, passing 'The Triple Crown' public house. After 250 years of service as 'The Tulip' it was recently renamed by the brewery in one of their regular fits of modernisation. Opposite are high iron gates which mark the old entrance to the rugby ground. Strangely the players do not drink here: Richmond use 'The Sun' while London Scottish use 'The Orange Tree.'

Access is probably easiest from the main road. Parking is usually along the driveway or around the back of the health club. On busy match days an overflow park is also behind the second team pitch and

goes parallel to the road. The Richmond Athletic Association (RAA), who run the whole complex, reckon that eight hundred cars can park with ease. In the days when Premiership matches took place each week and crowds of many thousands witnessed play, it was always a simple task to enter and park at the RAG.

The area of the RAG is but a fraction of the green land both sides of the river which make up Old Deer Park and Syon Park. To the north of the Richmond Rugby Club's ground is a golf driving range and slightly to the left is the top of the tall pagoda which dominates the southern part of the Royal Botanic Gardens at Kew.

The RAA already have in progress detailed plans to demolish the range and to build a new five thousand seat stand and clubhouse with the front facing south. With the knowledge that the rugby club are bouncing back from whence they came it is anticipated that the new structure (which has the full support of their Crown Agents landlord) will be ready in four years time.

Since Richmond's disgraceful expulsion from the top flight, many of the temporary seasonal structures have been removed. For example, the 5500 seater stand along the northern boundary has gone, as have the various sponsors' marquees and viewing structures which dominated the eastern end behind the goal.

In their place is now a concrete walkway, although some signs of the old order are still left. Everywhere are fire extinguishers, even out in the open. There are waste bins at each corner and security is the order of the day at all of the various gates.

On the eastern boundary is a health club gymnasium and beside it the store for groundsmen's equipment. Both are two storey with the dining area of the gym having large windows which spectators still use on match days. The store has a big balcony with dozens of teak tables and chairs which provides a comfortable viewing area.

Both north and west sides are now just used by people who like to stand near to the play. On the southern side is the 1970s concrete stand which has accommodation for 2500 in comfort on the rows of wooden seating. The view from here is perfect, as all corners can be seen with ease and the floodlighting for night games is excellent. The evening view over to the right shows the inside upper rooms of the rows of packed terraced Victorian housing: the taste of the occupants is heart-warming.

Next to the stand is the old pavilion, so old it has a preservation order on it. Downstairs is used as changing rooms for those playing on all of the other rugby pitches, while upstairs are the RAA offices. In between the two buildings is a covered entrance way where there are six pay-boxes. Nothing so crude as turnstiles here.

On the expansive outside wall to the left, but still under shelter, are two large honour boards. Alas, these reflect the names of the very many players of both clubs who did not return following various wars.

Just along from here is the rugby club office and next to it is the entrance to the splendid club shop. With Richmond having been demoted nine divisions you might have expected the enthusiasm to buy club items to have waned. None of it. This shop is outstanding with varieties of clothing and goods of all shapes and sizes. It took me fully twenty minutes to appreciate what was on offer.

Catering at rugby clubs around the country varies enormously. However, I challenge anyone to find anything better than that to be found at Richmond. I could spend numerous paragraphs describing the superb food available for both diners and general patrons. It varies from full breakfasts to seafood dishes, steaks, chicken, lasagne, and offers the best sausages to be found on the circuit. If you have never eaten here then make it one of your

RICHMOND /LONDON SCOTTISH   83%

How the Athletic Ground rates...

Access:	8
Car Parking:	8
Staff Attitude:	9
Comfort & Cleanliness:	7
Programme:	7
Catering:	10
Scenery & Surroundings:	9
Bars:	8
Club Shop:	10
Viewing & Shelter:	7
Total:	83 %
Ranking:	6th

ADDRESS: The Athletic Ground, Kew Foot Road, Richmond, Surrey, TW9 2SS.

DIRECTIONS: Leave the M4 (Junction 1) and follow the A205 and then the A307 to the roundabout at the junction with the A316. The Athletic Ground lies on the North side of the A316 just West of Richmond Circus roundabout and adjacent to Royal Mid Surrey Golf Club and the swimming pool, Pools on the Park. The nearest Underground/Railway Station is at Richmond.

PARKING: 800 spaces available.

TELEPHONE:
Richmond: 020-8332-7112
London Scottish: 020-8940-7156

WEBSITES:
www.richmondfc.co.uk
www.londonscottish.com

things to do for the future. I cannot praise the caterers more highly.

There are two main bars. Both are large enough to take five hundred drinkers in each, with two lots of two hundred being able to sit down. The members' bar has the added attraction of being stuffed full of memorabilia, much of which is on display behind glass in cases all along one wall.

The Richmond matchday programme is still on a parallel to that of premiership days. The adverts reflect the spending habits of club members and it is obvious that this is a club which will never be short of financial clout.

Priory Lane, Roehampton, London, SW15 5JH.

WHEN a rugby club was formed in Hampstead in 1879 they decided to call themselves after Rosslyn House which was situated on what is now Rosslyn Hill. This was how Rosslyn Park Rugby Football Club came into being, mainly due to the man who was its president for many years, CC Hoyer-Miller.

After somewhat of an early wandering life, which included playing in Hampstead and Gospel Oak, followed by sixty-three years at Old Deer Park, the site for a suitable home was eventually found by the junction of Roehampton Lane and Upper Richmond Road in the London suburb of Roehampton.

Much of the surrounding area makes you drool with envy. The property is of the highest calibre, spoilt only by blocks of ugly local authority built flats, some of whose occupants cause much heartache to the club's groundsman. However, with the erection of new gates in the driveway and closed-circuit television, the attention of these unwelcome visitors has been directed elsewhere.

In a walk around the immediate vicinity there can be found detached Victorian houses now worth well into seven figures and semi-detached worth not much less. This is one of London's most sought-after areas and any local estate agent is fortunate to have such property on their books. In fact, one agent produces a glossy magazine each month and always includes a rugby article in it, no doubt to impress prospective clients.

When the London Boroughs were created in the 1960s, the pen of the draughtsmen put the boundary of Wandsworth just the right side of the road for Rosslyn Park. The affluence and attitude of the Council has meant little (and, sometimes,

no) local taxation with the result that the club has been able to expand within the community.

All around are sporting organisations. To the north is the Roehampton Club, nowadays known for its squash players and in years past for the quality of its polo teams. Behind that is the Roehampton Tennis Club with both indoor and outdoor courts; and further back is Roehampton Golf Course. To the west of the rugby club are the extensive grounds of the Bank of England Sports Club (where my wife was once tennis champion for eleven consecutive years: it's amazing the trivia you read in these pages).

Opposite the ground is Barnes Common and on a day when the wind was in the right direction the noise from the football crowds at Craven Cottage could easily be heard: alas no more.

Spectator access can be obtained

from three sides of the ground, with vehicles having to use the Woking Close entrance off Priory Lane. There is a tarmacked car park at the rear and side of the clubhouse with overflow parking on the spare land at the eastern end and behind the northern stand.

The Priory Lane grounds might be situated by the side of one of South-West London's noisiest road junctions, but that does not stop a visitor from having a feeling of warmth and homeliness when walking around the pitch.

The main stand, which has seating under cover for 340 spectators, is on the northern boundary. To the left is stepped concrete terracing, with the trees behind providing adequate cover on a rainy day. To the right is low grass banking, with flat standing behind the posts at the eastern end.

A long covered terrace, with 352 seats, runs for virtually the length of the southern side parallel with Upper Richmond Road, while a large sponsors box is in the north-west corner. In front of the western-sited clubhouse are lawns, pathways and a roped barrier to keep onlookers away from the playing field. The club claim to have terrace accommodation for four thousand but this is probably a figure to satisfy the local Council, for in reality the ground could hold many more.

The club shop is in the far corner of the main clubhouse bar at the dining room end. On offer are the usual items of clothing but not in the wide variance of sizes found in the larger club stores. I was told by a committeeman that the best selling item is the club tie.

Near to the shop is the catering hatch and behind it the large kitchen. Here is where I had my main disappointment, for the selection of available food and the accompanying pleasant attitude seemed to have dropped somewhat sharply. In years past the hot food on offer at Rosslyn Park was known throughout the rugby world for its quality, quantity and most reasonable prices. I gather that the former kitchen manager retired last year and that catering has been taken over by an outside company. If the price of my cup of instant coffee is to be taken as a guideline then the profits for the season will be enormous.

All told there are four bars, with only one for the general public. The others are for members, sponsors and for the private use of the president and his invited guests. However, the large general bar is normally quite sufficient for spectators.

During my visit people could not have been more helpful, in particular the club's historian whose knowledge I found fascinating. He

How Priory Lane rates...

Access:	6
Car Parking:	6
Staff Attitude:	8
Comfort & Cleanliness:	6
Programme:	7
Catering:	3
Scenery & Surroundings:	8
Bars:	6
Club Shop:	5
Viewing & Shelter:	7
Total:	62 %
Ranking:	=41st

ADDRESS: Priory Lane, Roehampton, London, SW15 5JH.

DIRECTIONS: From the M3 follow the A316 and follow the signs for the South Circular Road A205. After passing signs for Richmond, stay in right hand lane over roundabout and turn onto A205 South Circular Road. Turn left at next traffic lights onto Upper Richmond Road West A205. Continue for approx. 1/2 mile and at next traffic lights turn right into Priory Lane. The entrance to the Ground is approx. 100 yards on the left.
The nearest Railway Station is Barnes.

PARKING: 200 spaces available at the ground.

TELEPHONE: 020-8876-6044

FAX: 020-8878-7527

CLUBHOUSE: 020-8876-1879

WEBSITE: www.rosslynpark.co.uk

demolished many club myths and his forthcoming 125-year history should be a publication well worth reading.

The amount of memorabilia scattered around is to be savoured. One area is dedicated to the 'Prince Obolensky Association' and honours the great man and his two historic 1936 international tries. But the star item is the painting which hangs above the door which leads to the President's Room. On a large canvas, the creator has detailed the important events in the life of the club. It is well worth viewing.

The matchday programme is only of sixteen pages yet it contains as much information as anyone would need. Printed on glossy paper it is a very good effort for this level of the game. What was nice to note was that programmes are produced for fixtures of the club's three other grade teams.

A visit to the Roehampton ground is a pleasant experience and a welcome is all but guaranteed. Continuing success on the playing field will see a very contented future for all concerned.

Millmoor, Masbrough Street, Rotherham, South Yorkshire, S60 1HR.

THE town of Rotherham has a history of which it should be proud. Founded in 937, it is now 1066 years old and has as its centre piece a glorious fifteenth century church which completely dominates the area. Designed by Thomas Scott, the Chancellor of England, he also added on a college in 1483. This was destroyed by Henry the Eighth.

On the hill above the church lies Clifton Park, fifty-six acres of land dominated by stunning flowers, among which are stand pillars and stones from the Roman town of Templeborough. To the south of the park lies Clifton Lane and by it the spiritual home of Rotherham Rugby Football Club.

Founded in 1923, the club had shared the ground with Rotherham Cricket Club in peaceful coexistence. Then success came to rugby and in order to meet the guidelines of the Premiership a move to the football club's ground had to occur.

At Clifton Lane, even during their previous top-flight tenure, the maximum crowd was 3,800 (versus Leicester) out of a 7,000 capacity. Now in a ground which holds 11,900 the average crowd is barely over 2,000. This means that two sides, the Family Stand and Railway End Terraces are never opened on match day. Do the Premier Rugby officials, stuck in their Twickenham towers, really think that thousands of cash-strapped South Yorkshiremen are suddenly going to appear on the terraces to see Sale, Wasps or Saracens?

Rotherham's only Premiership season was a huge learning curve. I attended their first game (versus Bristol) and found organised chaos. They had no concept of the needs of the media and were then still a club of regional leagues mentality. Things have had to change and with the cricket club unwilling to let rugby expand the only way to please the Premiership officials was to persuade the football club to agree to a ground-share.

So, the deed was done and from the beginning of last September rugby has been played at Millmoor, usually on a Sunday. Therefore this grounds report will be like Saracens, Wasps, Bristol and London Irish, all of whom now play on football pitches.

The ground is in the northern part of the inappropriately named suburb of New York (sic). It is surrounded on two sides by railway freight lines and is accessible from the east by Coronation Bridge.

It is the locals which strike you first on arrival. They dress in bargain clothes; live on cheap food and, if their general size is anything to go by, are part of the future diabetic time-bomb. I went to park in nearby Station Road (for the Millmoor car park is by ticket only) and got assailed by a man from the Pentecostal Church who said: "You can't park in this street. It's for disabled people only. Sport on Sunday is wicked." He then started singing religious songs at the top of his voice. You don't find too many like him at Harlequins.

The access points for rugby supporters are from Masbrough Street only. Should the day come when away fans need to be segregated then their entrance would be down the spooky Millmoor Lane where, like football fans, the police and stewards will search every intimate part of your body if they don't like the expression on your face.

Looking at the front entrance to the Millmoor ground, there is a public house on the left. The doors are guarded by some absolutely gorgeous bouncers, particularly the shorter one who has the unmistakable glint of lippy when he smiles. Then you have the club bar

which is called The Tivoli, a place I would frequent with the utmost caution until I was convinced that it was rugby folk inside.

To the right, past the turnstile entrances, is the club's portakabin match-day office and a temporary club shop. On my visit all club officials and stewards were most helpful, with one going out of his way to give me as much assistance as possible. He even gave me a personal conducted tour of the areas closed off for rugby.

You have to feel sorry for those in charge of the structure housing the club shop. On a wet day the puddles outside the portakabin are all in the wrong position for anyone wanting to enter. Once inside, the range is typical of what rugby clubs offer: fleeces, shirts, hats, scarves, sweaters and so on.

The catering I always find very acceptable for football, but you seem to expect more at rugby grounds and this is not the case. Having said that, the food and drink available inside Millmoor is of a good standard and fairly reasonable in price.

From the main stand and sponsors' boxes the view is of factories, factories and more factories. Go and stand on the northern terraces and the view is of factories, freight yards and waste land. To a student of industrial archaeology this place would be heaven.

The rugby supporters of Rotherham are light years away from their football counterparts and so must feel a sense of foreboding when standing on the Tivoli terraces. The comfort and clean-

ROTHERHAM 53%

How Millmoor rates...

Access:	6
Car Parking:	4
Staff Attitude:	8
Comfort & Cleanliness:	4
Programme:	6
Catering:	6
Scenery & Surroundings:	3
Bars:	3
Club Shop:	5
Viewing & Shelter:	8
Total:	53 %
Ranking:	49th

ADDRESS: Main office - Clifton Lane Sports Ground, Badsley Moor Lane, Clifton, Rotherham, S60 2SN.
Ground - Millmoor, Masbrough Street, Rotherham, S60 1HR.

DIRECTIONS: Exit M1 (Junction 34) take second exit, signposted Rotherham (A6109). Follow Meadow Bank Road approx. 1.5 miles, turn right at traffic lights onto Kimberworth Road. At T-Junction after approx. half a mile turn left over Centenary bridge to ground.
The nearest Railway Station is Rotherham.

PARKING: There is a large car park adjacent to the ground.

TELEPHONE: 01709-370763

WEBSITE: www.rrufc.org.uk/

liness expected by the round ball fans might not quite be what the oval ball supporters usually expect. Anyway, it's meant to be an improvement. No one, however, can complain about viewing and shelter, both of which are excellent all around the ground.

The newly-built pressbox is in a good position and comfortable enough for me to be able to read the programme before the match. Printed on glossy paper in decent colour the impression was of a publication with a bit too much advertising. My reading was continually interrupted by stewards rushing past to confront recalcitrant rugby fans who refuse to obey the rules about not smoking in a wooden stand.

The move to Millmoor has only been made to please rugby's hierarchy. It has not been made for the benefit of the club or its supporters. Playing to a seemingly empty house must be soul destroying for the players. Still, we are told this is progress. If it is, God help us all.

Heywood Road, Brooklands, Sale, Cheshire, M33 3WB.

A TRICK question asks: 'Which is the nearest football club to the River Mersey?' The answer is Stockport County. Ask the same question about rugby union and the correct reply will be Sale Rugby Football Club. Based in a now fashionable and trendy part of southern Greater Manchester, the Heywood Road club are still going strong in this, their 141st year.

Monty Barak in his centenary history described the locality at the turn of the last century as comprising 'artisan dwellings mixed with houses owned by the new monied middle-classes.' Now, those terraced houses are properties highly sought after by twenty-first century young professional couples.

A stroll around the area, serviced by the Brooklands tramlink, reveals a dormitory suburb of growing wealth, young children and quality schools. The cars parked in the narrow Groves and Mews reflect the tastes of the monied young most of whom also seem to need four-

Road to the south of the ground.

Then comes the main shock of the day and one which would be keenly felt by a regular football follower. The stewards were, collectively, the most helpful, charming, considerate and friendly group of people it has been my pleasure to meet. One (the man by the East Stand walkway at the Whitehall Road entrance) spoke to me about his role in such an understanding way that I would recommend him as an example to follow by many of those tin gods who strut their way around Premier League football grounds.

The programme sellers were situated at each entrance and the usual match supply of 1,500 were all sold by kick-off time. The forty-eight page glossy publication contained sixteen pages of advertisements, match reports, an article on recent changes in the laws of the game, a memory column (with, alas, errors of fact), club news and much more.

wheeled drive vehicles to take them to one of the proliferating local wine-merchants.

Car parking at the cosy Heywood Road ground is limited to just players and officials. However, on-street parking spaces are easy to find and it is safe to leave your car nearby and walk to the club through pleasant tree-lined thoroughfares. Numerous road signs indicating the way to the club are to be found on all nearby main roads. There are three entrances: through Heywood Road and the 'Little B' public house car park, both of which are off Marsland Road, and Whitehall

By the main gate is the Club Shop. The selection of replica shirts, fleeces, anoraks, caps and other pieces of clothing were varied and of good quality although if, like me, you are not of regulation size then disappointment may occur. One item for which Sale must be praised is their annual Handbook. Edited by the Club's Media Manager, this publication should be repeated by all of the other Premiership clubs as it is both useful and informative particularly about the team and its players.

Walking around the ground was a pleasure. The stewards passed the time of day as I absorbed the atmosphere and found that there was a tree lined view from every corner. "It's lovely working here," said one of them. "The trees make such a restful background." I could not agree more.

The main North Grandstand has seating for around two thousand patrons and runs for most of the length of the field. Opposite, the Jim Birtles Stand and other open terracing takes the same figure with the uncovered East Stand temporary seating absorbing just under a thousand. Behind the western end is the clubhouse with the first storey area being a dining and viewing area for the club's sponsors. The only slight inconvenience to the spectator would possibly be the lack of range of the floodlights into the far corners of the pitch but this is a pedantic comment.

Catering was very routine. The clubhouse had a small corner area which sold hot-dogs, pies, sausage rolls and hot drinks. A portable burger van by the Birtles Stand was dispensing greasy looking food at London prices, the appeal of which had me walking briskly in the opposite direction. Steer clear if you have a weight problem or are diabetic: the nutritional value was nil.

The main bar for use by the ordinary spectator was situated in the clubhouse. It was cramped yet friendly although after the game it was heaving with supporters of both teams trying to get in a pint or two before they had to leave. There were two other bars around the ground but they were for committee people, club members and sponsors.

The last of our sections comes in two parts: comfort and cleanliness. Taking the latter first, I was very impressed with the toilet facilities for women and the disabled. They were clean, tidy and efficient. I also liked the good sized room set aside for the players' wives and children. Maybe, one day, a creche might follow.

The main complaint comes last and concerns spectator comfort and enjoyment. How on earth can it be justified in having the volume of the sound system so loud that you cannot be heard by your neighbour even when facing him and shouting? No way is such grossly offensive noise enjoyable especially when you see spectators holding their ears in either pain or sheer discomfort. It so happened that there was a doctor next to my neighbour and he commented that the music being broadcast was so

SALE   68%

How Heywood Road rates...

Access:	8
Car Parking:	8
Staff Attitude:	10
Comfort & Cleanliness:	3
Programme:	6
Catering:	4
Scenery & Surroundings:	8
Bars:	6
Club Shop:	8
Viewing & Shelter:	7
Total:	68 %
Ranking:	=32nd

ADDRESS: Heywood Road, Brooklands, Sale, Cheshire, M33 3WB.

DIRECTIONS: Leave the M60 (Junction 8) and take the A6144 Old Hall Road. Continue clockwise round the one way system into Marsland Road. Pass the Sale Hotel on your left. Pass Little B pub on your left. Immediately turn into Heywood Road.
The nearest Metrolink station is Brooklands.

PARKING: On-street parking nearby.

TELEPHONE: 0161-283-1861

FAX: 0161-969-4124

TICKET DETAILS: 08712-220-120

WEBSITE: www.salesharks.co.uk

loud that "it could bring on a sufferers' epileptic fit at any time." The reality is that such a repugnant din causes damage to people's ears, but I suppose that the presenter of such a racket is beyond control and will continue to make spectators suffer in this way.

Generally a visit to Sale is to be savoured and enjoyed: that is, except for the noise.

(For the 2003/04 season, the club intend playing their first-team matches at Edgley Park, the home of Stockport County FC.)

Vicarage Road Stadium, Watford, Hertfordshire, WD18 OEP.

IT seems hardly any time ago that we were watching Saracens play on a north London park pitch at the Bramley Sports Ground. Those were the days when a crowd of fifteen hundred was about the safety limit and that figure was only reached on the odd occasion.

Nowadays the club play at the Vicarage Road Stadium in Watford and attendances into five figures are quite normal. This sea change has come about through professional people investing in the club and keeping faith along a somewhat rocky road. The move, via the now demolished Southbury Road Ground in Enfield, has established Saracens as one of the big-hitters in the new professional world of rugby union.

By sharing a ground with Watford Football Club, the stadium is, by necessity, somewhat utilitarian. Gone is the club atmosphere created so easily at Bramley Road: in its place the more corporate attitudes of the modern era. However, the success the club has had in integrating itself into the

South Hertfordshire community is a credit to the backroom staff. Various initiatives through schools and other local rugby clubs shows just what can be done if you try.

This is a report of a rugby club in, essentially, a football ground. It is viewed through the eyes of an ordinary rugby punter although, as was explained to me by the Chief Steward, there are different rules in place for each sport played at the stadium.

Vicarage Road is served by three railway stations. Two are on the Euston line (fast trains service Watford Junction with a slow service stopping at Watford High Street) with the Underground line terminating at Watford. This latter station is on the Metropolitan Line, made famous by the poetry of Sir John Betjeman, who eulogised in verse the mid-wars suburban expansion along the railway track. His 'Metroland' can be clearly seen on the Watford line and even more so as you walk along Cassiobury Park Avenue. Cross the Rickmansworth Road into West Watford and your walk to the ground becomes a complete contradiction in terms for the population is mainly Muslim. And who were the enemies of the Saracens during the crusades......

Anyway, I am diverting from the ground report. To attend a match by car is not a recommended exercise for there is car parking only for sponsors and officials. These are sited in the grounds of the next door Watford General Hospital or at the bottom of the delightfully named Occupation Road by the entrance to the allotments. For others, street parking might mean a walk of anything up to a mile if you can find a vacant place in the maze of terraced streets.

Access to the stadium is by way of twenty-one turnstiles or, for the disabled, three special entrances. The facilities for disabled people are excellent with their viewing areas first class, all of which include individual chairs for their carers. The special toilet facilities were superbly designed, well stocked and spotlessly clean.

Quite often I hear of football ground stewards not being able (or wanting) to adapt to the rugby codes being played at their grounds: Charlton Athletic and Bradford City being two which come readily to mind. However, I was most pleasantly surprised to find the stewards at Watford to be more than helpful, particularly the Chief Steward and the steward in charge of the Rookery End Stand. Both explained their role and also told me of how they monitor crowd safety and control. The attitudes were polite and commendable.

The main club shop is situated in Vicarage Road and forms part of the

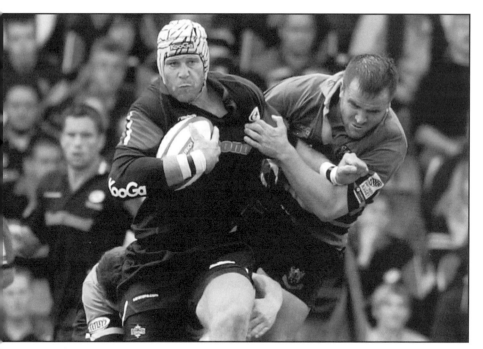

back of the Stand. On a Saracens match day the shop is fully given over to rugby. On sale were the usual selection of tops, shirts, tracksuits, scarves and bobble-hats. The sizes were standard but nothing in the dimensions suitable for an ageing prop forward going to seed. There was also a book on the history of the club which at a quick glance appeared to be quite informative. A second, smaller, shop was situated inside the ground in the Rous Stand.

The match programme was available from numerous vendors all around the ground. Priced at £2.50, it comprised sixty-four glossy pages of which twenty-five were either advertisements or illustrations. It is not one of the better Premiership programmes and as last season wore on the repetitive nature of the text actually became boring. Maybe this season will be different.

The ground is an all-seater stadium although there is still a small part of the East Stand (unused) in which the old terracing remains. This Stand was due for demolition last summer but the demise of ITV digital and the consequent loss of income to football clubs has resulted in Watford Football Club cancelling the project. Worse still, they have sold the ground and are now paying rent for being there. Where this leaves Saracens in the long term is anyone's guess.

SARACENS 62%

How Vicarage Road rates...

Access:	8
Car Parking:	3
Staff Attitude:	8
Comfort & Cleanliness:	7
Programme:	5
Catering:	6
Scenery & Surroundings:	3
Bars:	7
Club Shop:	7
Viewing & Shelter:	8
Total:	62 %
Ranking:	=41st

ADDRESS: Ground - Vicarage Road Stadium, Watford, Hertfordshire, WD18 0EP. Office - Rigby House, 34 The Parade, High Street, Watford, Hertfordshire, WD17 1EA.

DIRECTIONS: Leave M1 (Junction 5) and follow signs to Watford Town Centre. Join the ring road in the middle lane, moving into the left lane after the second set of lights and follow the signs to the Hospital and West Watford. Follow the mini one-way system around the pedestrian precinct, continuing straight up Vicarage Road where you will see the stadium on your left.

PARKING: Parking, by ticket only, is available at Watford General Hospital. On-street parking is difficult.

TELEPHONE: 01923-475222

FAX: 01923-475275

TICKET DETAILS: 01923-475222

WEBSITE: www.saracens.com

The capacity is 20,800 and it was not that long ago that over 19,500 turned up for a Saracens match. Everyone can sit in comfort with a number of executive boxes, hospitality areas and dining rooms lining one part of the Rous Stand, which makes up the western part of the stadium. Probably 80% of all spectators are under cover whichever part of the ground they are in at the time.

All areas are well served by bars, most of which have a variety of beers and spirits available. The other refreshment outlets sell the type of food and soft drinks which are not recommended by your dietician. Having said that, it was pleasant to see a number of machines dispensing Cadbury chocolate bars around the place.

If ever a spectator was to fall ill during a game, not only would help be on hand very quickly but all first aid facilities were noted to be of a very high standard.

Watford Football Club and Saracens, their tenants, have made a considerable effort in making the ground at Vicarage Road as user friendly as possible. It is just a shame that the area around the stadium is so morbidly dull and uninteresting.

SEDGLEY PARK

Park Lane, Whitefield, Manchester, M45 7DZ.

THE northern Manchester suburb of Sedgley Park is hardly any distance from the city centre. However, the ground of the club bearing its name is situated a couple of miles further up along the Bury New Road in the area known as Whitefield.

The suburb is a fascinating place and is set in what were the grounds of Sedgley House. It is mainly middle-class early post-war housing and has a large Jewish population.

These residents are mainly Hasidic: this is a sect of Jewish mystics which was founded in Poland two and a half centuries ago. They are characterised by their religious zeal and a spirit of prayer, joy and charity.

To see them on their holy day in their fierce black overcoats and wide-brimmed black hats is to watch a piece of ethnic culture so different to accepted principles. Because of this they are not involved on a Saturday with the sporting club of their area.

Just a short distance away is Sedgley Park Rugby Football Club situated off Park Lane, an appropriately named street as it is in part of one of the most expensive areas of Manchester. With the nearest council estate some ten minutes drive away there is very little burglary of nearby houses and the club suffers only minor, usually mindless, vandalism.

At the south-west corner of the ground is a gate which leads on to a road which becomes the driveway to Phillips Park Hall and Local Nature Reserve. I'm not sure about the tranquillity aspect as the M62 motorway carves right through the Reserve. To the right of the Hall's entrance are three full size rugby pitches for the club's other teams. These three become nine on Sundays when the hugely popular mini-leagues take over.

Behind the northern part of the complex is Whitefield Golf Course which stretches around the eastern boundary. A pond at the back of this terrace provides youngsters with a distraction as they can throw stones into it to while the time away as their fathers behind them cheer on the players.

Entry for both cars and spectators is by the main gate off Park Road with around two hundred parking spaces inside the ground. A pebbled track goes around the outside of the spectator areas to allow access for vehicles. However, I was deeply disturbed on my visit to have one speeding car, driven by a player, force me into a bush and to witness another whipping around while play was in progress. This is unacceptable behaviour and should not be tolerated.

The ground capacity is 2500 of which there are 312 seats in the main stand. There is concrete terracing all along the eastern side and at its southern end are various old lorry containers which have been adapted for the groundsman's vehicles and equipment. Also along here, at the boundary, someone years ago had the foresight to plant pine trees as future windbreaks. They are now most effective in their chosen task as well as filtering noise from the motorway.

From the top of the stand, which is situated in the middle of the western terracing, there is a glorious view over the Irwell valley towards Heaton Park. At times the carriages on the Metrolink tramway glint in the dying afternoon sun as they carry their passengers over the high embankments of Prestwich. On a cold day, by the stairs to the stand, a large trestle table groans with big thermos flasks full of much refreshment. 'Hot Toddys £2' says a welcoming sign.

The clubhouse takes up the whole of the northern part of the ground. It is a two-storey structure which had a major extension built some twelve years ago. There are three upstairs bar areas of which one is in the major function room which caters for around one hundred and fifty diners. The catering was splendid at the meal I attended. I had a look into the kitchens and saw that they were spotlessly clean.

The second bar is situated in the middle of the building and has ample room as well as large sliding windows which open on to a large balcony. Quite a few spectators watch the match from this vantage point albeit behind the goal. The tea-bar is situated between the bar and the club shop so the options are open for these fans to easily grab a hot drink while a place kick is being prepared and lose none of the action.

The club shop is very well stocked and one of the two ladies in charge said: "If there is something you want which is not available in your size then we can easily get it made for you." She did not have to worry for all the items I looked at would easily have fitted me, some with room to spare! The range of goods went from home-and-away kits through to ties, waterproof jackets, key-rings, fleeces, badges, beanies and much more. Stock sizes ranged from children's to triple extra-large.

The walls of this room and the third bar were covered with memorabilia. One large glass case

SEDGLEY PARK   79%

How Park Lane rates...

Access:	7
Car Parking:	7
Staff Attitude:	10
Comfort & Cleanliness:	8
Programme:	7
Catering:	8
Scenery & Surroundings:	8
Bars:	8
Club Shop:	9
Viewing & Shelter:	7
Total:	79 %
Ranking:	=9th

ADDRESS: Park Lane, Whitefield, Manchester, M45 7DZ.

DIRECTIONS: Leave M60 (Junction 17) and take the A56 heading towards Bury. Keep in the left hand lane to filter past Aldi/McDonalds and continue past Whitefield Golf Club. Turn left at the lights on to Park Lane. Follow this road, going straight across a mini-roundabout. The Club is 200 yards further on your left. The nearest Metrolink station is Besses o 'th' Barn.

PARKING: 200 inside the ground.

TELEPHONE: 0161-766-5050

WEBSITE: www.sprufc.com

was full of items relating to Bob Kimmins who played for England, Lancashire, Orrell and Sedgley Park. The latter bar is known as 'The Frank Hardman Lounge' in memory of the late Lancashire RFU president.

Two other items caught my eye. The first being the windows in this lounge most of which have the club badge and name beautifully inscribed on the glass; the second were two large wooden boards situated on the walls of the back stairs. They recorded the history of the club. Besides these was a small memorial board commemorating the lives of the six players who died in the second war.

The club programme comprised sixty-four pages of which forty-eight were a standard seasonal shell. The matchday insert of sixteen pages were very informative and pure editorial. What some of the more elderly members would have made of the news that the club's website has now recorded "over 60,000 homepage hits" is for some conjecture.

A day at Sedgley Park is most enjoyable. The natives are friendly and the camaraderie enticing: it is an effort to bid farewell.

Bridgnorth Road, Stourton, Stourbridge, West Midlands, DY7 6QZ.

STOURTON PARK is situated in South Staffordshire yet has a postal address of another county - the West Midlands. Confused? Not as much as I was when visiting this lovely rural rugby outpost.

On leaving the M5 motorway a road sign clearly stated 'Stourbridge 12 miles.' Eleven miles later (according to the mileometer in my car) a road sign said '6 miles.' For the next four miles along the A458,

all signs still said '6 miles.' Then (after fifteen miles) a sign said '4 miles,' so I knew I was getting nearer.

The Geographers' Map Company book confirmed that I was actually travelling west and not going around a very large round-about in a rugby-induced trance. Soon we got to a two and a half mile sign, and after twenty-two miles I had accomplished the so called twelve. I was in Stourbridge. Glory be!

My guide to everything in England told me that this was an industrial town of 56,000 souls. That may be the case today but Stourbridge is noted for its historic buildings and a strong connection with Samuel Johnson, known better by most as Dr Johnson, whose dictionary, published in 1755, preceded the birth of the rugby club by just 121 years.

Johnson taught at King Edward VI School in what is now the town centre and is said: "... to have spent many hours walking along The Ridge while composing his poems on classical themes." This long hill now has, on its western side, Stourton Park, the home of Stourbridge Rugby Football Club.

From the town the narrow Bridgnorth Road wends its way through the messy area of Wollaston and suddenly, on the invisible county boundary, greenery appears. Quickly the quality of the housing changes from grotty to gorgeous; the bend of the road down the slope catches you by surprise and there, on your left, is the welcome sign you have been waiting to read.

The club's driveway is shared with High Park Farm, two of whose employees treated us to a mid-afternoon version of an American Dumper Truck contest as they raced their farm vehicles around the outbuildings. Hand-brake turns from tractors do cause such an awful pong.

There is ample parking all around the ground. The main car park, split into three tarmacked sections, has one hundred and forty-three marked spaces with a gravel overflow for one hundred and twenty, and then room for two hundred and thirty-five more on grass verges. Should this not be enough then space is available by the main road fencing for many more.

Over the road is another entrance, but this is to Stourbridge Lawn Tennis Club which is situated to the south of New Wood. Through it runs both the River Stour and the Stourbridge Canal. In days past when the rugby club was sharing with Stourbridge Cricket Club at Amblecote, a mile away, it was not unknown for spectators to arrive for a match on some of the several working industrial canal boats.

The views from the rugby ground take in much of the area, with the lush pastures showing numerous hues of green. Lambs gambolled in the fields; the northerly wind blew the long grass into patterns, and the hills were inviting enough for entwined lovers to be seen walking along the pathways.

Around the main ground are five other pitches, two of which are only suitable for younger players. Behind the northern banking is the third team pitch, while at the low southern end the training area slopes up to the farmhouse.

The modern West Stand has seating for four hundred and twenty spectators as well as having a ramp and ample room for disabled fans. Alas, on my visit, broken glass was strewn all over the ramp which would have made access difficult, if not dangerous, for any wheelchair occupant. A men's toilet was underneath the stand but nowhere was there any facility for half-time food or hot drinks to be obtained.

There were also seats in front of the clubhouse on the eastern side. Although uncovered, these two hundred and eighty-eight places on metal strips gave good views of the action on the pitch, so long as no one got over-excited and stood up.

The club moved to this ground in 1965, when it was officially opened, with the first phase of the clubhouse built in 1981. The latest phase was completed only a few months ago and included three extensions to the original building. However, one matter needs attention: the clock on the high wall was running three and a quarter hours slow. It so reminded me of the Spike Milligan book 'Puckoon' in which the village clock was right twice a day.

The building runs for about two-thirds the length of the pitch and on the downstairs level there are various changing rooms, three deep baths, a fitness centre and some medical rooms. From the outside are entrances to the toilets, said by John Inverdale in his 'Daily Telegraph' column to be "the best rugby toilets in Britain." I wouldn't go that far but having not sampled them all I cannot give an opinion.

On the upstairs level are three bar areas. The first you reach is the 'President's Room' which is used by sponsors on match days for around seventy diners. The 'Members' Bar' holds around a hundred people and this is where most of the club photographs and plaques are to be found decorating the walls.

The main bar room also serves as a dining area and the snack meals available were basic but of excellent quality. A new large kitchen was included in the recent development and its cleanliness is to be commended. Over one hundred can dine in comfort without interfering with the drinkers by the bar.

Other areas, such as the 'Tower Room', also provide smaller places for sponsors and even let them have their own private balcony viewing. Another space is used for selling club-embossed clothing but the selection on offer was rather poor.

Not so the match programme, expertly put together by Vernon Davies, the club's press officer. Comprising fifty-six glossy pages it

STOURBRIDGE   65%

How Stourton Park rates...

Access:	6
Car Parking:	7
Staff Attitude:	7
Comfort & Cleanliness:	6
Programme:	8
Catering:	5
Scenery & Surroundings:	10
Bars:	6
Club Shop:	3
Viewing & Shelter:	7
Total:	65 %
Ranking:	=39th

ADDRESS: Bridgnorth Road, Stourton, Stourbridge, West Midlands, DY7 6QZ.

DIRECTIONS: The ground is situated on the A458 (Bridgnorth road), two miles west of Stourbridge town centre.
The nearest Railway Station is Stourbridge Junction.

PARKING: Space for 500 cars.

TELEPHONE: 01384-393889

WEBSITE: www.stourbridge-rugby.com

is as professional a production as could be wished, with plenty of news and historical features.

I was fortunate that the time of my visit coincided with a typical spring day. It gave the arboreal nature of the ground a warmth and a feel-good factor. I hope it stays that way.

TYNEDALE

THE Romans loved it around Cumbria and Northumberland. In fact Emperor Hadrian, on one of his regular visits to the area in 117 AD, two years after he came to the throne, ordered a wall to be built. It was no ordinary wall: it ran from the Solway Firth in the east to the mouth of the River Tyne in the west.

It took the incredibly quick time of four years to build (well, slave labour does work a bit quicker than unionised workers) and its intention was to act as a defence against the marauding North British tribes. The resultant towns along the way included Corbridge [Corstopitum], the current home of Tynedale Rugby Football Club.

The best route from the south is to leave the Great North Road just after Scotch Corner and go along the old Roman road known as Dere Street. The engineering of these roads two thousand years ago was a remarkable feat, for even today driving up and down the hills of County Durham needs considerable concentration.

The scenery is spectacular, even more so as you enter Northumberland. Once over the River Derwent and Kiln Pit Hill it is a downhill run towards the Tyne Valley. On the day of my visit I encountered the Tynedale Hunt. They had started in Dipton Wood and followed the scent westwards.

Modern life and the main road had distracted them but how the contrast hit me. Here were riders young and old (including a lovely little girl, dressed in the correct manner and riding her pony) supported by hunt followers enjoying a centuries old traditional sport. Meanwhile, white-wine drinking diners at trendy city dinner parties had for years been trying their best to deprive these people of their homes, their work and their futures. It is all so odious.

Suddenly I was in Corbridge, a small town of considerable charm with its ancient church, walled gardens and medieval buildings. Situated on a hill to the north of the River Tyne this town attracts tourists even in the heart of winter. The single lane bridge over the river was built 325 years ago and is still in perfect order.

After crossing it, turn to the left and in front of you is Corbridge railway station. The old station building is now called 'Valley' and is an Indian restaurant. Eating at tables on the platform watching trains to Newcastle, Sunderland and Carlisle pass by must be quite a novelty.

A tree-lined driveway takes you to the entrance which is by the main pitch. To the left is the training ground with its floodlights blending into the trees. By the side is a hardstanding area for thirty cars. Opposite, three hundred and fifty cars can park on gravel while the grassland by the side of the railway line could take about two thousand vehicles.

This amount might seem excessive but it has to be explained that in 1976 the club moved here to what were once the grounds of the Tynedale Agricultural Society. Now, each May Bank Holiday, the site is used to host the Northumberland County Show and with an average of twenty-thousand visitors the car spaces are needed.

The single storey clubhouse is situated on the western side of the huge compound with the main stand on the southern edge with its back to the railway line. There seem to be pitches as far as the eye can see looking east and north. On the day of my visit all of them were being used.

The main stand was built in 1992

and opened by the then RFU president Danie Serfontein. It has wooden seating for 576 spectators, with a ramp and a designated section for disabled supporters. There is no other shelter, with the three other open sides having just concrete or grass walkways along wooden perimeter posts.

The views all around were magnificent. I kept asking myself how many variations of the word 'wonderful' I could use in this piece to describe the beauty of the place. The calm and tranquillity of the surrounds were broken by the occasional trains passing by and the drone in the far distance of a plane landing at Newcastle Airport.

At the club's northern boundary is the ground of Corbridge Cricket Club. Its gabled roof pavilion sits in front of lengthy flood prevention banking which runs as far as the eye can see. Over the top was the River Tyne, its banks dotted with anglers who were not having exactly the most successful of days.

Around the back were various stone-built cottages and modern bungalows. Every driveway had at least three vehicles sitting in them. I asked a passing resident the cost of such buildings. He said: "These are in the £350,000 bracket but around here you do get a fair bit of land with each house."

The clubhouse is in two main parts. The northern half comprises eight changing rooms with three substantial old-fashioned communal baths and a dozen showers. In the centre is a large hall off which is the secretary's office. On the wall of the hall are three plaques: two of which honour the seventy-six club members lost in both wars. The third, and those in the adjoining bars, refer to past players and officials.

The sponsors' bar and dining area face on to the playing field, while the public bar and players' eating section are at the rear. Before the match I tried to purchase a lunch but was twice refused for no apparent reason. Others appeared to be more successful. It took three attempts to get a cup of coffee, although I was lucky enough to be able to obtain a bread roll. Some time after the game had ended a hatchway opened and those in the know were able to buy pasties. It was all so strange.

I kept asking about a club shop and was continually informed that items would be put on show "shortly". I saw what the club had to offer in a glass-covered wall display. These included shirts, shorts, ties, socks, hats and beanies, all of which carried the club's crest.

Although only of sixteen pages, the programme was an excellent effort containing reams of news and detail. In a mass of editorial I saw only one literal error and none in

TYNEDALE   73%

How Tynedale Park rates...

Access:	9
Car Parking:	9
Staff Attitude:	7
Comfort & Cleanliness:	9
Programme:	8
Catering:	4
Scenery & Surroundings:	10
Bars:	7
Club Shop:	2
Viewing & Shelter:	8
Total:	73 %
Ranking:	=21st

ADDRESS: Tynedale Park, Station Road, Corbridge, Northumberland, NE45 5AY.

DIRECTIONS: From the A69 westbound head for the roundabout at the south side of the bridge over the River Tyne. Take the turn off signposted Prudhoe A695. After approx. 200 metres take the slip road to the left signposted "Station". Continue along Station Road for 100 metres and the entrance to the ground is on the left. The nearest Railway Station is Corbridge.

PARKING: Ample parking at the ground.

TELEPHONE: 01434-632997

FAX; 01434-632996

WEBSITE: www.tynedalerfc.com

'Come On Tyyyyyne!' the club's magazine.

Tynedale Park is one of the most scenic grounds a rugby supporter can visit. People were friendly and helpful, yet it was obvious that attention to detail was lacking in a number of ways. Hopefully, it may well improve.

College Grove, Eastmoor Road, Wakefield, West Yorkshire, WF1 3RR.

THE name of the town of Wakefield became known to history students as the place where, in 1460, the Yorkists and Lancastrians fought a bloody battle. The War of the Roses was in full swing when the two sides fought in a blinding snowstorm south of the town. Mannygates Lane has a monument showing where the Duke of York fell in the fight and today, just around the corner, is the ground where Wakefield Wildcats Rugby League Football Club fulfil their fixtures.

In later years Wakefield enjoyed being the capital of the West Riding and became known for its great wool market. The splendid county hall with its gabled bays and octagonal tower has, on the pillars of the arcaded balcony, seven statues in niches. These represent the wealth of the area which were gained from coal-mining, iron-founding, spinning, glass-blowing, agriculture, engineering and pottery.

The new and emerging middle-classes of the late nineteenth century tended to build their homes to the north of the town in what are now spacious plots of land and near to two good standard schools. It was a natural area for a rugby union club to develop.

College Grove is an arboreal street enhanced by houses with large bay windows and high ceilings whose night time internal lighting throws a collective glow over the road and into what is now the Wakefield Sports Club. Sitting in the pressbox on a mild late summer evening, I found that the match in progress was given an extra warmth by the radiance coming from rows of living room bulbs all unencumbered by closed curtains. Above one Wakefield scrum my eye caught what appeared to be a family quarrel over the dinner table: we will never know what happened next.

There appear to be five sports played at the complex with rugby union taking top slot. This is followed by hockey (on a pitch equal to international standard), bowls, squash and rifle & pistol shooting.

Early arrivals can take advantage of the hundred or so car spaces but, even if you are too late to benefit from the admirable matchday parking organisation, plenty of on-street spaces can be found opposite along St John's Grove and Belgrave Mount and Terrace. The residents I spoke with had no objection to spectator parking and car vandalism was an unknown subject in this part of the town.

Access to the ground is by local knowledge, a good map book or by chance sighting of either of the two council provided signs which state blandly 'Wakefield RUFC' with an accompanying arrow. In contrast, the road signs for directions to the rugby league ground are measured in their dozens and are usually on the main traffic boards. The dichotomy is marked.

There are two entrances to the club's ground, one from College Grove View at the back of the main stand side, with the other being along the main driveway. No crude turnstiles here: just a pleasant welcome and the opportunity to buy a programme at the same time. The voluntary effort that went into the issue I purchased was a credit to both club and editor.

Just before the entrance was the main Club Shop. Actually the name is a misnomer as it is a shop mainly for the Wakefield Hockey Club with rugby having one small rack for replica shirts and another for a pile of books on the history of the club. The manager was helpful and informative explaining that hockey sticks alone accounted for ninety-five percent of his sales.

Various signs then invite the spectator to enjoy a drink at the shared sports club bar or to partake

of a snack or a meal provided by the kitchen.

Well! What a menu. What a choice. Whoever does the catering here is a hero. The food on offer is of a quality that would make a number of restaurants proud to be able to provide for their hungry patrons. Visiting southern spectators gawked at the selections of food in front of them and then, when paying for their food, actually asked the cashier if she was charging them the correct price. The word bargain came to mind. Where else today would you get a superb meal for just two one pound coins?

However, on the negative side I found certain attitudes amongst people I presumed to be either club officials or their hangers-on to be not quite what one would have expected. The requests such as: "Could you let us have the teams for tonight, please" being a point in question. When spectators are also

WAKEFIELD 60%

How College Grove rates...

Access:	5
Car Parking:	6
Staff Attitude:	4
Comfort & Cleanliness:	5
Programme:	7
Catering:	10
Scenery & Surroundings:	8
Bars:	5
Club Shop:	3
Viewing & Shelter:	7
Total:	60 %
Ranking:	45th

ADDRESS: College Grove, Eastmoor Road, Wakefield, West Yorkshire, WF1 3RR.

DIRECTIONS: Leave M1 (Junction 41) and take A650 to Wakefield. At the third roundabout turn right for Wakefield and left at first lights. At the next lights turn left and at T junction turn left. Follow road round right hand bend, Wakefield Sports complex is on the right.

PARKING: 100 spaces at the ground and on-street parking nearby.

TELEPHONE: 01924-374801

FAX: 01924-290069

treated with such disdain it makes for some embarrassment.

A walk around the ground before the game showed that the club had made an effort regarding spectator viewing and shelter. The main (south) covered stand ran along part of one touchline and opposite a temporary-permanent open stand went from corner to corner. The seating was comfortable although a bit basic, although open seat patrons got a little damp when drizzle arrived just before half-time which signalled an early departure by many to the club bar. A balcony behind one goal seemed to be for executive guests with the far (western) end offering nothing except a railing upon which to lean.

From a comfort aspect a seat in the covered stand would be the limit of any expectations. The ground was clean and tidy but with normally unexciting attendance figures to record no plans for any expansion would need to be considered for the foreseeable future.

There is no real criticism to make about a normal run-of-the-mill rugby club. The praise must go to the caterer: his sausages were magnificent.

St Anthony's Road, Blundellsands, Liverpool, L23 8TW.

THERE are times when you are totally unprepared for the surprise a visit to a new venue can bring. Some grounds are little short of tips while others have a utilitarian purpose: some are good in parts, while others take your breath away. The Waterloo ground at Blundellsands falls into this last category.

I did not know what to expect as I drove through the West Lancashire countryside. Soon I was skirting the city of Liverpool and going past the Aintree racecourse. Being the nosey sort I had to drive down the Melling Road; look at the trickle of water called Becher's Brook, and drive up the entrance road to admire the massive grandstand. I had no idea that the Leeds & Liverpool Canal ran along the course.

Curiosity satisfied, it was then

only a short journey to the furthest north-eastern edge of the Merseyside conurbation at Crosby. Here the suburbs become more middle-class and detached houses are the norm. Independent schools proliferate, with eleven being within walking distance of each other. The whole area has a feel of wanting to stay together.

The area of Crosby known as Blundellsands looks as if it was mainly developed towards the latter part of the reign of Queen Victoria. Along the sea front and just behind it are the huge houses so loved by the wealthy of a century ago. A few streets further inland and you come to their smaller equivalents of the mid-wars era. When these houses are demolished in the name of progress, anything up to a dozen new dwellings take their place: all tastefully built, of course.

Drive down St Anthony's Road and at the end is the entrance to Waterloo Rugby Football Club. Inside the ground is enough space for all to park their vehicles in comfort. However, there are those who like street parking and, other than the areas marked out by the club placing yellow cones along the kerbing, there is room for everyone.

The men on the gate were helpful and gave me much information. I found out that one of them was an assistant press officer at Liverpool Football Club, who always volun-teers his services when his round ball team are not playing.

I chatted with them and to some of the committeemen who joined us. I said that I had noted that all of the surrounding houses had external lights and burglar alarms on their walls. Was there a problem? The response shook me. "My house has CCTV as well as alarms which go off when people enter the garden," said Marketing Director Peter Edwards. "My cars also have tracking devices installed in them. You are not that far away from the villains here," he added. Others told me similar stories. When I looked at the map book I could see what they meant.

The entrance opens up to become a driveway once inside the gates, with the Club Shop on the left and parking spaces opposite. In the shop the items on offer are the usual fare but the majority of stock has to be kept elsewhere for obvious reasons.

A large grassed mound lies in the centre of the ever-widening approach, with white brickwork around its perimeter. In the centre is a tall flagpole from which the club flag flutters proudly. At the base is a plaque which reads: 'Presented by H.P.Lumby & family in memory of John Lumby killed in action 1st September 1942'.

A right turn takes you along the uncovered southern terrace. It is built in local stone and is slightly steeper than usual. This gives the spectators at the top of the pack an excellent view over the whole of the playing surface. It also subjects them to the cold wind which blows in from Liverpool Bay.

Walking around the ground and looking at the views from all angles it was hard to believe you were actually in Liverpool. Behind the main stand is the practice pitch and along the back of the western end runs the Lime Street to Southport railway line. Trains every ten minutes in both directions are hardly noticed. The quietness and tranquillity of the affluent suburb was refreshing.

On entering the six-thousand capacity ground the first thing that hits you is the splendid wooden grandstand. Its design is most sensible, cut away at each end to taper towards extended corners in order to give spectators a perfect view. I am told that a brand new stand is to replace this one during the summer. I hope its style is as well thought out.

Curving around behind the western goalposts are the gymnasium, sponsors' area, general bars, a players' bar and changing rooms, and four ground-floor flats. There is also a food bar at the front along with a large kitchen behind.

The flats are used by club players, usually those from overseas, and have their own small garden. The concept is brilliant: does this happen elsewhere? With a gymnasium on site there is surely no excuse for any fitness problems.

The whole of the mock Tudor clubhouse is truly magnificent. With the club steeped in history and having been a major force until recent times, every room is a rugby museum in its own right. What was placed upon shelves; behind glass in cabinets; covering every available piece of wall space and even on mantlepieces, was truly breath-taking. So enraptured did I become with all of these treasures that time flew past and I nearly missed the start of the match.

The match programme is edited and produced by Geoff Lightfoot Media. It is of thirty-six pages, printed on glossy paper and is of good value. Some of the articles were thought-provoking and the layout was in an easy to read style.

Waterloo is a wonderful club to visit. The friendliness is catching and the atmosphere of the place is a reminder of those innocent days of yesteryear. If you haven't had a Saturday in Blundellsands then try to do so as soon as possible.

WATERLOO   82%

How Blundellsands rates...

Access:	8
Car Parking:	9
Staff Attitude:	9
Comfort & Cleanliness:	9
Programme:	8
Catering:	7
Scenery & Surroundings:	9
Bars:	8
Club Shop:	6
Viewing & Shelter:	9
Total:	82 %
Ranking:	7th

ADDRESS: St Anthony's Road,
Blundellsands, Liverpool, L23 8TW.

DIRECTIONS: At junction with M57/58,
take A5036 West towards Crosby and
Docks. Turn right at first traffic lights (by
police station). Immediately bear right on
main road around perimeter of housing
estate. Straight ahead at first lights then
left at second lights towards Liverpool
A565. Though lights and several pedestrian crossings, turn right at roundabout,
through housing estate, turn left at T
junction then immediately right and bear
right. Straight ahead at roundabout along
St.Michael's Road to cross roads by Church.
The ground is 100 yards on right.
The nearest Railway Station are Hall Road
or Blundellsands & Crosby.

PARKING: Limited parking available at the
ground.

TELEPHONE: 0151-924-4552

Wharfeside Avenue, Threshfield, North Yorkshire, BD23 5ND.

WHEN I die and go to heaven will it be any better than going to Wharfeside Avenue, home of Wharfedale Rugby Football Club? I have often mused upon this question, normally after having spent a day at the club and mixing with the folk around it.

North Yorkshire is a delightful part of the world, even more so when you are in the Wharfedale part of the Yorkshire Dales National Park. The towns to the immediate south, Ilkley and Otley, are old Roman garrison settlements and the invaders from twenty centuries ago liked nothing better than to wander up the Wharfe valley and to construct a few buildings.

Following on from this, places such as the priory which is Bolton Abbey came to pass as the district moved into the civilising process we know today. The advent of the railways opened up large tracts of the Dales only for the government of forty years ago to close them down.

Nowadays the only way to get to Grassington is by one of four routes which, on a typical Saturday afternoon, are blocked by car loads of visitors who insist on driving at twenty miles an hour in the middle of the road.

Threshfield is an eastern extension of Grassington, situated over the bridge which spans the River Wharfe. It is fairly wide and fast flowing at this point of its course, and its beauty is breath-taking. A right turn takes you into Wharfeside Avenue: go past the new houses in Badger Gate and a few hundred yards down the road is the entrance to the rugby club.

Here you encounter your first problem, for manning the gate are people so affable and chatty that by the time you have parked your car and gone back to collect a programme you have already made new friends. When I mentioned this to a committeeman later in the day he immediately replied: "The stewards here are to welcome people to the club," a philosophy, incidentally, of which many associ-ation football organisations are totally unaware.

The friendliness is infectious as I found when opening the door to the clubhouse. On a match day it is the policy of the club to have an official in-situ to meet and greet all visitors. No one had any idea who I was yet I was given a quick resume of what was available for my comfort and pleasure.

The clubhouse was built in 1995, and officially opened later that year by David Duckham. It has been designed with taste in mind and is certainly no run of the mill structure. The upstairs floor has a landing, to the left of which is a large open room used for sponsors and guests. The other room is the members' bar.

Both have been constructed in a light pine timber with the former having an arched ceiling with pine struts. This gives a feeling of air, light and space added to which is the complementing pine furniture. The specially designed carpet is red with WRUFC green and white logos in patterns along it. Like most clubs the walls, both up and downstairs, are covered in honour boards or with commemorative shirts and plaques.

The ground floor is a perfect design. A refreshment bar is just inside the front door with a large menu from which to choose your hot food. Other than the usual pies and sandwiches there were varying snack meals, with the one recom-mended to me by a visiting journalist being the "hot chunky steak pie, chips, peas and gravy" for

a price so ridiculously low that if I mentioned it you probably wouldn't believe me. There is also a special children's menu.

As you enter the main bar, on your right is the players' dining room which is used mainly by women with children before and during the game. Around to the right is a general dining area situated far enough away from the bar for people to enjoy a quiet drink with their snacks. The bar itself has a high ceiling so the room does not get stuffy or give the impression of being claustrophobic when packed.

The club shop is situated by the doors which lead out to the main stand. I found that by the time I had noted down on my pad what was available virtually a page had been used. The selection of clothing is huge with particular emphasis being given to children's sizes. Umbrellas, hats, ties, teddy bears and other ephemeral items were available.

The main stand, situated on the northern side of the ground, has only 115 seats yet it was not full during the match as the vast majority of spectators preferred to stand. Opposite is covered concrete terracing which takes up a large

How Wharfeside Avenue rates...

Access:	8
Car Parking:	8
Staff Attitude:	10
Comfort & Cleanliness:	9
Programme:	8
Catering:	9
Scenery & Surroundings:	10
Bars:	8
Club Shop:	8
Viewing & Shelter:	8
Total:	86 %
Ranking:	4th

ADDRESS: Wharfeside Avenue, Threshfield, North Yorkshire, BD23 5ND.

DIRECTIONS: Take B6256 from Skipton bypass, signed Grassington. After eight miles turn right just after Old Hall Inn in Threshfield, left after 500 yards along Wharfeside Avenue.

PARKING: 120 spaces within the ground.

TELEPHONE: 01756-752547

FAX: 01756-720257

WEBSITE: www.wharfedalerugby.co.uk

part of the southern boundary. Behind the western goal is a typical Dales stone wall while the eastern end is just railings after which is the driveway.

Cars were parked all around. Some went on to the half-sized junior pitch at the south; one hundred and twenty were on the tarmac by the clubhouse; others went on to the second-team pitch while more straggled the driveway and the long Wharfeside Avenue.

Walking around the ground provides breath taking views of the River Wharfe, its valley and hills; Bastow Wood and its nature reserve. From the stand, looking left, you can see the rolling slopes of Kimpergill Hill but, of even more significance, down in the valley is yet another rugby pitch.

The programme, on its front cover, shows the yellow truck which ferries the players to and from this far off pitch. To watch forty or so burly men going up and down ladders from this vehicle brings home the true meaning of the sport of rugby union.

Long may the attitude and ambience of Wharfedale Rugby Football Club exist, for this is as near to the sport's utopia as you will come.

Sixways, Pershore Lane, Hindlip, Worcester, WR3 8ZE.

A FEW years ago, when I was working on match days for the football side of the BSkyB satellite television company, one of my colleagues was employed at the same time as a sports presenter for BBC Hereford & Worcester radio station.

He lived in the area and I remember his views about the town. "Worcester is a wonderful place in which to live," he said. "It is central to everywhere in the country and no one is further than a couple of miles of so from the motorway. Travelling around by car is so easy."

It is also a delight to travel to Worcester by train from London. After Oxford the line becomes a single track and meanders through the north of the county before going through the Cotswold Hills, crossing the Vale of Evesham, and ending up on the plains of the River Severn.

In years past, alighting at Foregate Street meant a short walk to the old rugby ground, but no more. Now it is a special match-day bus service or a taxi ride out to Sixways on the north-east fringes of the town. There you come across the magnificent new home of Worcester Rugby Football Club.

Being away from the centre of things, albeit on a junction of the M6 motorway, there are no places nearby to eat or drink before a game. On the day of my visit public houses in The Shambles, Friar Street and Trinity Street were full of lunchtime drinkers, most of whom appeared to be preparing themselves for the match ahead.

I wandered down to New Road, just across the river, where the county cricket team were on display in a setting as beautiful as could be created. A few hundred yards away is Worcester Racecourse, said to "offer the lowest level of spectator satisfaction to be found anywhere on the British racing circuit." In the equivalent articles to these on cricket and horse racing the rankings for Worcester were nearly top and completely bottom. I did wonder how Sixways would fare in comparison, but I need not have worried.

The complex sits on a 40-acre site with the main entrance abutting Pershore Lane. On a match day those without passes for the executive car parks, which take 564 vehicles, are directed along a gravel road to the back of the fourth pitch. Here another thousand or so cars plus coaches can park with ease.

The second and third pitches, which are situated behind the North Stand, both have floodlights and covered terracing. In fact there is more shelter and comfort for spectators here than on the main grounds of two other clubs in the same league! Further north, behind a row of trees, are twelve more pitches, albeit some of them mini size for junior age groups.

There are six main entrances, all situated along a tarmacked driveway leading from the main road. Two wooden huts act as ticket collection points and by the way the gates were designed there is absolutely no queuing needed to get into the ground. In wandering around and asking questions I found that a number of the gatemen actually subscribed to *Rugby Times*. One of them mentioned my intended movements into his walkie-talkie and after that everywhere I went I was greeted like a long lost friend.

Once inside the ground I was truly amazed by the efficient and professional attitude adopted by all of those who were so busy on a match day. The club generate 55% of their income from non-rugby related sources - and it is easy to see why.

The clubhouse, situated around part of the main West Stand, is an airy building designed with comfort in mind. Inside, the high first-floor ceilings let the sun pour into the rooms which immediately give a warming effect, even on a cold day. On this level are sponsors' dining areas, the 'International Bar' which is for members' use, and the huge 'Hallmark Suite' which is for dining. Comfort is a byword here.

On the ground floor is the largest of the club's ten bars. In it a side hatch dispenses all sorts of hot and cold food and drinks. It is in a corner of this room where the club's main memorabilia is situated behind glass in wall-mounted cases. A doorway leads into a permanent marquee where a hot lunch was available to all and sundry without any need for a booking. An extension for the use of sponsors held over 150 diners. This area is where regular boxing evenings take place.

There are two Club Shops in the building, a small one open only on a match day and another, much larger, one to the rear of the building. There was a seemingly enormous offering of clothing, both on wall racks and on stands. Other items included beanies, mouse-mats, pencil sharpeners, rulers and numerous other items with the club's logo attached. There were even piles of Rugby Times on all counters.

Further around the back of the stand is the Indoor Training Centre. This facility is quite amazing for not only were there fitness, training and treatment rooms but an indoor sanded pitch occupied over sixteen thousand square feet!

The West Stand had 625 bucket seats with the pressbox at the rear. Above is a long television gantry which shows how prepared the club is for that final step into the big time.

The South Stand is a splendidly-designed building. There are 1250 seats on the ground level above which are 34 executive boxes which hold another 550 spectators. The ground floor entrance to the boxes looks just like a hotel reception area and all the Worcester match-day staff were neatly attired in business wear. Behind the stand is a well stocked medical room.

The East Stand has 1364 seats, all of which are under cover while the North Stand has open seating facilities for another 990 fans. Access to this stand is by walkways over a stream, the name of which seems to have escaped everybody's notice.

All around the ground are various temporary bars and burger vans, most of which were paired in

WORCESTER 91%

How Sixways rates...

Access:	10
Car Parking:	10
Staff Attitude:	10
Comfort & Cleanliness:	9
Programme:	9
Catering:	8
Scenery & Surroundings:	9
Bars:	8
Club Shop:	9
Viewing & Shelter:	9
Total:	91 %
Ranking:	1st

ADDRESS: Sixways, Pershore Lane, Hindlip, Worcester, WR3 8ZE.

DIRECTIONS: Leave M5 (Junction 6) take the road to Droitwich (signposted Rugby Centre), the Club is 400 yards on the left.

PARKING: Unlimited within the ground.

TELEPHONE: 01905-454183

FAX: 01905-459333

CLUB SHOP: 01905-459308

WEBSITE: www.wrfc.co.uk

the four corners. There were also programme booths, but the one thing I did not find was the reputed skittles alley: maybe it was in use as a sponsor's dining area.

The views from all around the ground were of the splendid local countryside. There was no motorway noise which augers well for the forthcoming classical concert being held on the main pitch by the Liverpool Philharmonic Orchestra.

The match programme is a top-quality publication. Printed on 64 glossy pages, 28 of which are advertising, it gives a feel of being well prepared after some detailed planning. There was a lot of club news and information all in an easy to read layout.

Worcester Rugby Football Club is as professional and advanced a sporting organisation as could be wished. They are without question the template for other clubs to aspire. If there were more clubs like this in the rugby world then we really would be living in paradise.

TOP CLUBS BY CATEGORY

EASE OF ACCESS

Leicester, Worcester 10

Bridgend, Melrose, Northampton, Otley,
Tynedale 9

Doncaster, Gloucester, Harlequins, Leeds,
Llanelli, London Irish, London Welsh, Lydney,
Newbury, Newcastle, Oxford Univ, Richmond,
Sale, Saracens, Waterloo, Wharfedale..........8

Bath, Blackheath, Boroughmuir, Cambridge
Univ, Coventry, Esher, Jed-Forest, Manchester,
Orrell, Pontypridd, Sedgley Park 7

Bracknell, Bristol, Glasgow, Halifax, Kendal,
London Wasps, Neath, Rosslyn Park,
Rotherham, Stourbridge, Wasps 6

Harrogate, Nottingham, Plymouth,
Wakefield...5

Edinburgh 4

CAR PARKING

Worcester 10

Bridgend, London Irish, Lydney, Melrose,
Newbury, Newcastle, Otley, Tynedale,
Waterloo 9

Boroughmuir, Bracknell, Doncaster, Esher,
Leicester, Llanelli, Northampton, Richmond,
Sale, Wharfedale 8

Bedford, Blackheath, Halifax, Harlequins, Jed-
Forest, Leeds, Manchester, Nottingham, Orrell,
Pontypridd, Sedgley Park, Stourbridge........7

Cambridge Univ, Edinburgh, Glasgow,
Harrogate, London Wasps, London Welsh,
Oxford Univ, Rosslyn Park, Wakefield 6

Bath, Bristol, Coventry, Gloucester, Kendal,
Plymouth 5

Rotherham 4

Neath, Saracens 3

STAFF ATITUDE

Blackheath, Halifax, Lydney, Melrose,
Newcastle, Orrell, Sale, Sedgley Park,
Wharfedale, Worcester 10

Bedford, Boroughmuir, Bridgend, Doncaster,
Glasgow, Gloucester, Harrogate, Llanelli,
London Welsh, Newbury, Northampton, Otley,
Richmond, Waterloo 9

Cambridge Univ, Coventry, Jed-Forest, Kendal,
Leicester, Manchester, Nottingham, Oxford
Univ, Pontypridd, Rosslyn Park, Rotherham,
Saracens 8

Esher, London Wasps, Plymouth, Stourbridge,
Tynedale 7

Bath, Bracknell, Harlequins,
London Irish 6

Leeds..5

Neath, Wakefield......................................4

Bristol 3

Edinburgh 1

COMFORT & CLEANLINESS

Blackheath 10

Cambridge Univ, Northampton, Tynedale,
Waterloo, Wharfedale, Worcester...............9

Bedford, Gloucester, Harrogate, Leicester,
Llanelli, London Irish, London Wasps, London
Welsh, Lydney, Manchester, Melrose, Oxford
Univ, Sedgley Park 8

Doncaster, Esher, Glasgow, Halifax,
Harlequins, Jed-Forest, Leeds, Newbury,
Newcastle, Orrell, Pontypridd, Richmond,
Saracens 7

Bath, Boroughmuir, Bracknell, Bridgend,
Coventry, Edinburgh, Kendal, Neath, Rosslyn
Park, Stourbridge 6

Nottingham, Otley, Wakefield 5

Bristol, Plymouth, Rotherham 4

Sale...3

PROGRAMME

Leicester 10

Harlequins, London Irish, London Welsh,
Otley, Worcester 9

Bath, Blackheath, Doncaster, Gloucester,
Halifax, Kendal, Melrose, Neath,
Northampton, Plymouth, Stourbridge,
Tynedale, Waterloo, Wharfedale 8

Bedford, Bristol, Glasgow, Nottingham,
Richmond, Rosslyn Park, Sedgley Park,
Wakefield 7

Cambridge Univ, Coventry, Esher, Harrogate,
Jed-Forest, Leeds, London Wasps, Lydney,
Newbury, Newcastle, Pontypridd, Rotherham,
Sale...6

Boroughmuir, Llanelli, Orrell, Oxford Univ,
Saracens 5

Bracknell, Bridgend..................................4

Manchester 3

Edinburgh 0

CATERING

Harlequins, Leicester, Llanelli, Manchester,
Richmond, Wakefield 10

Cambridge Univ, Doncaster, London Welsh,
Newcastle, Northampton, Wharfedale 9

Boroughmuir, Bristol, Gloucester, Harrogate,
London Wasps, Melrose, Otley, Sedgley Park,
Worcester..8

Bath, Bedford, Bridgend, Coventry, Glasgow,
Newbury, Orrell, Waterloo..........................7

Blackheath, Bracknell, Halifax, Jed-Forest,
Kendal, Leeds, Plymouth, Rotherham,
Saracens 6

Esher, London Irish, Pontypridd,
Stourbridge 5

Lydney, Neath, Nottingham, Sale,
Tynedale 4

Rosslyn Park..3

Edinburgh 2

Oxford Univ 0

SCENERY & SURROUNDINGS

Bath, Cambridge Univ, Jed-Forest, London
Welsh, Manchester, Melrose, Stourbridge,
Tynedale, Wharfedale 10

Glasgow, Newbury, Otley, Richmond, Waterloo,
Worcester 9

Bedford, Blackheath, Gloucester, London
Wasps, Newcastle, Oxford Univ, Pontypridd,
Rosslyn Park, Sale, Sedgley Park,
Wakefield 8

Boroughmuir, Bracknell, Bristol, Doncaster,
Halifax, Harrogate, Leicester, Lydney 7

Coventry, Edinburgh, Esher, Harlequins,
Kendal, Neath, Northampton, Orrell 6

Leeds, Llanelli, Nottingham 5

Bridgend, London Irish, Plymouth 4

Rotherham, Saracens 3

BARS

Harlequins, Leeds, Leicester, Pontypridd 9

Glasgow, Llanelli, London Welsh, Lydney,
Manchester, Melrose, Plymouth, Richmond,
Sedgley Park, Waterloo, Wharfedale,
Worcester 8

Bath, Blackheath, Boroughmuir, Bridgend,
Bristol, Cambridge Univ, Coventry, Esher,
Gloucester, Harrogate, Jed-Forest, Kendal,
London Wasps, Newbury, Newcastle,
Northampton, Orrell, Otley, Saracens,
Tynedale 7

Bedford, Bracknell, Doncaster, Halifax,
London Irish, Nottingham, Oxford Univ,
Rosslyn Park, Sale, Stourbridge 6

Wakefield 5

Edinburgh 4

Neath, Rotherham 3

CLUB SHOP

Harrogate, Leicester, Melrose, Northampton,
Richmond 10

Bath, Coventry, Llanelli, London Irish,
Sedgley Park, Worcester 9

Blackheath, Gloucester, Halifax, Harlequins,
Kendal, Leeds, Neath, Newbury, Nottingham,
Otley, Plymouth, Sale, Wharfedale...............8

Bridgend, Doncaster, London Welsh,
Newcastle, Oxford Univ, Saracens 7

Bedford, Bristol, Esher, London Wasps,
Manchester, Pontypridd, Waterloo..............6

Orrell, Rosslyn Park, Rotherham 5

Bracknell, Cambridge Univ, Edinburgh........4

Boroughmuir, Glasgow, Lydney, Stourbridge,
Wakefield 3

Jed-Forest, Tynedale 2

VIEWING & SHELTER

Northampton 10

London Irish, Oxford Univ, Waterloo,
Worcester..9

Bedford, Bridgend, Bristol, Cambridge Univ,
Glasgow, Gloucester, Harlequins, Harrogate,
Leicester, Llanelli, London Wasps, Lydney,
Manchester, Melrose, Orrell, Rotherham,
Saracens, Tynedale, Wharfedale 8

Blackheath, Doncaster, Esher, Jed-Forest,
Leeds, Newbury, Newcastle, Otley, Pontypridd,
Richmond, Rosslyn Park, Sale, Sedgley Park,
Stourbridge, Wakefield...........................7

Bath, Boroughmuir, Bracknell, Coventry,
Halifax, Kendal, Neath, Nottingham 6

London Welsh..5

Edinburgh, Plymouth 4